GRRRRR

A Collection of Poems About Bears

Edited by CB Follett

Arctos Press, Sausalito, California

GRRRRR
A Collection of Poems About Bears
A HoBear Publication

ARCTOS  PRESS
P.O. Box 401
Sausalito, CA 94966-401
CB Follett: Editor/Publisher

Cover Art: *Please don't endanger my species,* photograph by Dr. Alessandra DeClario
Title Calligraphy: Jo Ann Burchfiel, *Letters & Images*

Book Design: Christi Payne & CB Follett
Typography: Christi Payne, Book Arts

Library of Congress Cataloging-in-Publication Data
Follett, CB
     GRRRRR   First Edition

ISBN 0-9657015-1-4
Poetry 2. Bears—Poetry. 3. Animals—Bears—Poetry 4. Nature—Bears—Poetry 5. Myths—Bears—Poetry.

Library of Congress Catalog Card Number: 98-74911

This book is dedicated to
Earth and all who live on Her:
Respect, Balance, Peace.

And to Lee, who gives me all of those.

and with acknowledgment to
Teddy—age 73
Little White—age 55
Jonny Bear—age 28
Teddy Senior & Teddy Junior—age 5

who continue to bring comfort to our family

Acknowledgements

DC Berry: "Thinking Too Much: The Dancing Bear," *Divorce Boxing*, © 1998 Eastern Washington University Press.

Henry Beston: Epigraph from *The Outermost House* by Henry Beston, copyright 1928, 1949, 1956 by Henry Beston. © 1977 by Elizabeth C. Beston. Reprinted by permission of Henry Holt and Company, Inc.

William Borden: "Bear Warning," *1997 Minnesota Poetry Calendar*, © 1997 Black Hat Press.

Allen Braden: "Bear Poison," © 1994, *Southern Poetry Review*, Winter.

J. R. Brady: "I read that," excerpt from *Merging Traffic*, Eyelet Press 1995.

Barbara Brent Brower: "On a Night Without Moon," © 1999 *Arizona State Poetry Society Prize Anthology*.

Grace Butcher: "Night Visitor" appeared in the *Atlanta Review*, Spring 1999.

Hayden Carruth: "Bears at Raspberry Time" from *Collected Shorter Poems 1946-1991* © 1992 by Hayden Carruth. Reprinted by permission of Copper Canyon Press, PO Box 271, Port Townsend, WA 98368.

Robert M. Chute: "V. Balancing," *When Grandmother Decides to Die*, © 1989, Blackberry Press.

SuzAnne C. Cole: "Ursa Minor," © 1999, *Sunlight on the Moon*, Carpenter Gothic Publishers, Inc.

Billy Collins: "Flames," *The Apple That Astonished Paris*. Reprinted by permission of the University of Arkansas Press. Copyright © 1988 by Billy Collins.

Mary Crow: "As If," copyright © 1996 by Mary Crow. Reprinted from *I Have Tasted the Apple* with the permission of BOA Editions, Ltd., 260 East Avenue, Rochester, NY 14604.

Amy L. Dengler: "Ursa Major" has previously appeared in *Between Leap and Landing* from Folly Cove.

David Allan Evans: "Feeding the Bears," *Train Windows*, 1976, Ohio University Press.

Cathryn Essinger: "The Philosophy Professor Discusses the Nature of the Self-Conscious Mind" first appeared in *Poetry* 1996. It is reprinted from *A Desk in the Elephant House* by Cathryn Essinger, © 1997; with permission, Texas Tech University Press, Lubbock. 1-800-832-4042.

Sharon Fain: "Waiting for the Bear," *Times Ten: An Anthology of Northern California Poets*, 1997.

David Fisher: "The Bear" from his book *Teachings*, © 1977 by David Fisher, Back Roads.

Earl Fleming: Naturalist, quote beginning "It would be fitting ..."

CB Follett: "Bush League," *Spitball*, 1995 and "Winter Bears," *Xenophilia*, 1995.

Cynthia Gallaher: "White on White," *Zoo Poems*, Columbus Zoo/Pudding House Press.

J. Ruth Gendler: "how the bear came to me," *Creation*, Fall 1993.

Maria Mazziotti Gillan: "The Black Bear on My Neighbors' Lawn in New Jersey," *Things My Mother Told Me* by Maria Mazziotti Gillan (Toronto, Canada: Guernica Editions, 1999); reprinted by permission of Maria Mazziotti Gillan © 1998.

Taylor Graham: "Bear-Hunger" first appeared in *America*, reprinted in 1997 *Anthology of Magazine Verse & Yearbook of American Poetry*.

Rasma Haidri: "Bears," *Mothering*, No. 65, Fall/Winter 1992.

Jim Harrison: "My Friend the Bear" and "Bear" from *The Shape of the Journey: New & Collected Poems* © 1998 by Jim Harrison. Reprinted by permission of Copper Canyon Press, PO Box 271, Port Townsend, WA 98368.

Penny Harter: "Relic," © 1998 Penny Harter, is from *Lizard Light: Poems from the Earth*. Reprinted by permission of Sherman Asher Publishing.

Marie Henry: "Folsom Street Rain," *Poetry at the 33 Review*, Vol. 3.

Will Hochman: "Bears of Cheyenne Canyon" was first published in *Spring Magazine* and *A Writer's Choice*.

Jnana Hodson: "Primer for Bear," *Yakima*.

Ted Hughes: "The 59th Bear" from *Birthday Letters* by Ted Hughes. Copyright © 1998 by Ted Hughes. Reprinted by permission of Farrar, Straus & Giroux, Inc.

Ingrid Jeffries: "Apples and Bears" first appeared in *Her Day Begins Flamingo Pink*.

Paul Jenkins: "Well" from *Radio Tooth* © 1997 by Paul Jenkins, by permission of Four Way Books.

George Keithley: "In the Sky are Two Bears" and "The Burning Bear," both published in *The Burning Bear*, Heatherstone Press, Amherst, MA.

Galway Kinnell: "The Bear," from *Three Books*. Copyright © 1993 by Galway Kinnell. Reprinted by permission of Houghton Mifflin Co. Previously published in *Body Rags* (1967). All rights reserved.

David Kubach: "Fellow Travelers," first published in *The Wisconsin Academy Review* 1979, subsequently in *First Things*, copyright © by David Kubach, Holmgangers Press 1980, and in *Wisconsin Poetry*.

Maxine Kumin: "You Are in Bear Country," copyright © 1986 by Maxine Kumin, from *Selected Poems 1960-1990* by Maxine Kumin. Reprinted by permission of W. W. Norton & Company, Inc.

Gary Lawless: " I shot that bear . . ." and "Treat each bear as the last bear . . .," from *First Sight of Land*, copyright © 1990 by Gary Lawless, Blackberry Books.

Ursula K. LeGuin: "The Bear's Gift" from *Always Coming Home* © 1986 by Ursula K. LeGuin, first published by Harper & Row, New York.

Joan Logghe: "Outside Pagosa Springs," © 1999 by Joan Logghe, from *Blessed Resistance*, Mariposa Press.

Jeanne Lohmann: "Toward Morning the Inuit Grandmother Talks to Herself" first appeared in *Passages North*, also *Granite Under Water* © 1996 by Jeanne Lohmann.

Denise Low: "The Bear Emerges," *Poets At Large: 25 Poets in 25 Homes*, Helicon 9 Editions 1997.

Seán Mac Falls: "Ode to the Bear," *The Poets Corner*.

Elaine Magarrell: "The Truth About Bears" first appeared in *Yankee Magazine*, and was published in *On Hogback Mountain* by Elaine Magarell.

Pat Mangan: "The *Bear*," © 1998 by Pat Mangan from *The Harness* by Pat Mangan, used by permission of Four Way Books.

Judith McCombs: "The Man" has appeared in *Poetry Northwest, Bear Crossings, Sisters of the Earth* and *Against Nature: Wilderness Poems* by Judith McCombs published by Dustbooks.

Ken McCullough: "The Red and Black" first appeared in *The Iowa Source* 1996.

David Meuel: "Grizzly" first appeared in *Pegasus*.

A. Milne: "Furry Bear," by A. A. Milne, from *Now We Are Six* by A. A. Milne, illustrations by E. H. Shepard. Copyright 1927 by E. P. Dutton, renewed © 1955 by A. A. Milne. Used by permission of Dutton Children's Books, a division of Penguin Putnam Inc.

Judith Minty: "Last Bear Poem" appeared in *Poems for the Wild Earth*, Blackberry Books. "The Bear-Spring" appeared in *Yellow Dog Journal*, copyright © by Judith Minty, Parallax Press.

N. Scott Momaday: "The Bear," copyright © 1992 by N. Scott Momaday. From *In the Presence of the Sun* by N. Scott Momaday. Reprinted by permission of St. Martin's Press, Incorporated.

Miles David Moore: "The Bears of Paris," title poem of *The Bears of Paris*, copyright © 1995 by Miles David Moore, Word Works Capital Collection; *Pivot*, Number 41; and *Oxford Poetry*, Volume X, Number 1, Easter 1998.

John Muir: Naturalist, quote beginning "Bears are made of . . ."

John Murray: Naturalist, quote beginning "Those who have packed . . ."

Navajo: "Song of the Black Bear," *Anthropological Papers*, v.33, pt. 1:119, 1933, Courtesy of The American Museum of Natural History.

Duane Niatum: "The Black Bear" appeared in *Pacific Search Magazine*.

Sheila Nickerson: "When Spring Came and the Blue Bear Came to Town" appeared in *The Sky's Own Light*, Minatour Press.

Mary Oliver: "Winter Sleep" from *Twelve Moons* by Mary Oliver. Copyright © 1977 by Mary Oliver; first appeared in *Poetry Northwest*. By permission of Little, Brown and Company.

With thanks to the following for assistance and support: ↄ

Special thanks to Susan Terris,

as well as Marilynn Geiger, Ruth Daigon, Lee Follett, Bill Noble, Christi Payne, Armando Quintero, Deborah Daishow Ruth, Tracy Stephenson.

Douglas Long, Department of Ornithology and Mammalogy, California Academy of Science for providing information on the taxonomy of bears.

John Smelcer for Native American myth synopses used on section title pages and his statement for the back cover.

Dr. David Graber, National Park Service scientist, for his statement on the back cover.

The following members of SSILA, the Society for the Study of the Indigenous Languages of the Americas for their help in the listing of the word "bear" as rendered in many of the languages of the North Americas: Judith Berman, Robert Brightman, Lynn Burley, Harold Crook, Christopher Culy, Kim Dammers, Ives Goddard, Robert Gomez, Joseph Grimes, Ruth Holmes, Darin Howe, Philip LeSourd, Don Macnaughtan, Lisa Mitten, L.M. Morgan, Richard Mueller, Jean Mulder, Randi Nott, John O'Meara, Richard Rhodes, Kevin Rottet, Blair Rudes, Susan Steele, Gillian Story, Marie-Lucie Tarpent, Akira Yamamoto, and especially to Marie-Lucie Tarpent, who contacted her colleagues and coordinated the resulting information, and furthermore put up with a flood of questions.

Thanks for suggestions:
Hannah Ackerman. Pam Bernard, Allen Braden, Barbara Brent Brower, Grace Butcher, SuzAnne Cole, Lee Cooper, Laura Corsiglia, Lisa Couturier, Dancing Bear, Donna Dean (Black Wolf), Mark DeCarteret, David Allan Evans, Margaret Evans, Lyn Ferguson, Charles Finn, Cynthia Gallaher, Dan Gerber, Maria Mazziotti Gillan, Pamela Gray, John Gribble, Rasma Haidri, Mary F. Haynes, Marie Henry, Jane Hilberry, Marjory Kent Jacobs, Robin Jacobson, D. Jane Johnson, William Keener, George Keithley, Diane Kendig, Gary Lawless, Joan Logghe, Jeanne Lohmann, Leza Lowitz, Diane Lynch, Seán Mac Falls, Joan Maiers, Judith McCombs, James McGowan, Miles David Moore, Diane Nicolson, June Owens, Kathy Pearce-Lewis, Arnold Perrin, Kenneth Pobo, Martha Rhodes, Melanie Richards, Carmela Ruby, William Rudolph, Deborah Ruth, Dorothy Ryan, Thom Schramm, John Smelcer, Laura Snyder, Soldier Blue, Hannah Stein, Tracy Stephenson, Alison Townsend, Susan Terris, Kay Van Natta, Nan Wishner, Paula Yup, Kristin Camitta Zimet

And thanks to the artists, and all the poets who sent their poems for consideration.

N.B. Bears are a popular subject for poems. There are many bear poems besides those included in *Grrrr,* and poets who write about bears often have several on the subject. For those interested in more bear poems, look for *Bear Crossings, An Anthology of North American Poets* edited by Anne Newman and Julie Suk, The New South Company, 1983.

Ursa Major and *Ursa Minor,* the constellations of the night sky have derived from bear myths of ancient times and from many cultures. The Greek version is of Kalisto who had a son, Arcas, by Zeus. In anger, his wife Hera turned Kalisto into a she-bear and Arcas became a hunter. Once, he had his mother in range and his arrow notched. Zeus, taking pity, threw them into the sky by their tails, which is why the sky bears have long tails. In other cultures the tail stars are three braves who track the great bears forever. Each autumn they kill the bears with arrows, and the spilling blood stains the leaves red and orange. The trees drop their leaves in mourning. Then each spring, the sky bears are reborn and the braves set out after them again.

Contents

All That Is Left Is To Name Him
Central Yupik myth

a drum beat, a heart beat
Dena'ina myth

To Kill The Distance Between
Tanacross myth

Waiting For The Bear
Cheyenne & Crow myth

Treat Each Bear As The Last Bear
Inũpiaq myth

Illustrations

CB Follett ☙

WE NEED ANOTHER and a wiser and perhaps a more mystical concept of animals. Remote from universal nature, and living by complicated artifice, man in civilization surveys the creature through the glass of his knowledge and sees thereby a feather magnified and the whole image in distortion. We patronize them for their incompleteness, for their tragic fate of having taken form so far below ourselves. And therein we err, and greatly err. For the animal cannot be measured by man. In a world older and more complete than ours they move finished and complete, gifted with extensions of the senses we have lost or never attained, living by voices we shall never hear. They are not brethren, they are not underlings; they are other nations, caught with ourselves in the net of life and time, fellow prisoners of the splendour and travail of the earth.

Henry Beston, The Outermost House

The Truth About Bears

THE ESKIMO suddenly stopped. Far out across the pack ice something was moving toward him. The hunter watched for a long time until finally he saw that it was a Ten-Footed Polar Bear! Quickly, he released the dead seal he had been dragging and ran as fast as he could towards his village, still carrying his long spear. When the great bear was upon him, the Eskimo threw his spear with all his strength, killing the beast. He cut off all ten feet, but no one in his village believed they came from one polar bear.

—from a Yupik myth

The Truth About Bears

The old bear plays a game much like quoits;
he splashes water rings over the lake.

Slim trout rise to rub noses with air;
the tracks they leave are round as moons.

The old bear waits for the fish that is strong,
rash, obsessed with the meaning of bear.

When the strong fish springs like a trap from the lake
his tail strikes the bear with the strength of ten fish.

The force of the fish hits the bear
like the brush of a wing or the scratch of a twig.

The bear strikes the fish with the strength of one bear.
For a moment the bear holds the fish in his mouth

alive. Fish against fur is paler than berries
before they burn blue. In the eye of the fish

is the truth about bears.

The Fisherman

I stepped into the river.
As the downstream rush
      swept around me
I braced myself against it
and eyed the quiet pools
along the opposite shore.
The morning was so alive,
      clean, sharp-edged
      and perfect . . .

The bear stepped into the river
from the other bank
about 40 yards upstream
looking for the same fish
I'd tied my perfect flies
      to catch.

Dark brown and tipped with gold
he rippled like the water's surface.
      Massive, competent
he lumbered into the swift current
which for him
      might as well have been made
        of air.

He glanced downstream,
gave me a regal, unruffled stare
and turned his attention
      to the early salmon.

In a smooth,
      powerful move
his paw sliced through the water,
separated a fish
from its riverworld

and tossed it up
                on the bank —
the first of several trophies
he was to carry away
that morning.

Calm,
        unhurried,
                he took his due . . .

Watching him
        blended flawlessly with his realm
                dominant by right
I could almost understand
the desire people have
to bend their knees
before those they believe
are born to rule.

The Black Bear

When black bear's paw
is a net across the Elwha,
we watch its stroke draw
light from the backs of salmon.

When black bear's paw
is the sculptor of the river,
we are the spirits of the rapids,
eat their song for the salt.

Fishing for Grizzlies

Along a white-watered branch
of the Clark Fork River,

fly-rod in one hand,
my dog's leash in the other

I see the warning sign:
Danger: Beware of Grizzly Bears.

I stop and listen, look
both ways like I'm crossing

a busy city street, a boulevard
buzzing with diesel fumes and cars.

But no, this is Montana,
home of the grizzly bear, mascot

for the state, the university,
myth-made motto for a way of life:

eat or be eaten, don't run,
learn to play dead.

Christ, I'm not fishing for trout,
I'm fishing for grizzlies!

My dog the live bait,
my arm – my whole body –

the pole to fight
the pull of that beast,

to be dragged
kicking and screaming

a minnowy man-child
into that fanged-toothed mouth.

Bear-Hunger

I was sleeping when they came.
I slept in the savor of pot roast,
the woolish warmth of wood-stove,
and the long night's moon measuring
my dreams.

       But in the morning
I found their prints
stitching the old orchard,
circling each tree. They lifted
bear-bulk for the hanging apples,
the ones too poor to pick.

And so I reached, too,
and plucked just one,
and bit it to its seeds.
The flesh was sweet
but scant. It tasted
like hunger.

the montana grizzlies

nothing can keep them away
from the hard yellow kernels

fool's gold on the railroad
tracks, ten-thousand tons

of spilled corn only a bear
can smell. Even after

the tracks are cleared
by armies of vacuums

even after an electric fence
is erected, even after

the corn-riddled rock
and dirt are scooped out

even after seven bears
and a nursing cub

are killed by trains
they come, they find

more corn, they come
to feast on it, some

of it fermented, they
stagger drunk, sway

crookedly back
to their caves

they keep coming
to the railroad tracks

continued on next page

along Bear Autumn Creek
they gather together

like a town meeting,
their massive brown black

velvet bodies glistening
in the early morning sun

nothing will stop them
the craving takes over

the craving blinds them, drives
them forward, the craving

is their master, the craving
is god

Ode to the Bear

Grizzled-brown sound of tuba walking
in the way of circles you wobble step, inverse,
as does a broken waltz, bearly graceful.

You sniff your way a crush alpine meadows
and making sense for you are lowly berries,
rude as any intruder might be in the foothills

of the Gods. "More wine for the great Polyphemus,"
say the drunk brambles, brighty doomed sailors
all a wash by behemothing jaws which hang

them over. Yet Ursa, if in minor you must play
by the cosmos stilted view, Great Major, it is they
who glare more distant, as if you really cared.

Wild Strawberries

In long gone, unplowed pasture, rolling
off the hillsides, the bear found them.

Crosslegged, slowly untangling, parting the dense
brown-green summer grasses, as if separating
fine hair, he carefully combed their spindly looping
beads, red flecks the size of a baby's finger-

                                nail &
                                small
                                er,

to the center of its clawed paw, cupping
& lapping the cool nubbins hollowed
paper-thin, sugar so pure
it stung his tongue,

sat back, innocent creature of delight
in mid-day sun, raising snout, eyes
closed to perfect blue, unclouded sky,

smacking perfect sweetness
again & again

to the roof of
his mouth.

The Biologist Examining Bear Tracks

Perhaps I've seen more bears,
real bears, padding their long
clawed way down Autumn's
frozen rivers following the foggy

breath of caribou. Perhaps I've
seen more sunlight glint on their
grizzled-gold faces through meadows
of waving yarrow. I've seen

their muzzles bloody in wolf-kill,
seen them excrete twigs after feasting
on blueberries. I've watched them
watching me through thin windows.

They follow my scent. I find
where their tracks enter
the river, where water drips
from their fur to fleck the stone.

I've counted salmon bones
by the stream. I know what they eat.
Their heads slowly wag side-to-side.
Shifting scents, rot and growth

equally alluring. Claws combing
talus for bulbs, for bitter roots.
Teeth tearing into diseased spruce,
tongues lolling sour pith for bugs.

Daylight finds me measuring
the seep of water into a muddy print.
I've lost my peripheral vision.
Nights I am dreamless, tired

continued on next page

from the exactitude of note taking.
I want to dream heart-cave-dreams,
listen with shaggy ears. There is more
than a measured heart-beat. More than

endless scatology. Locations of dens.
The tallying of birth and death.
The bear rises on its hind legs, watches me
follow its tracks into an alder thicket.

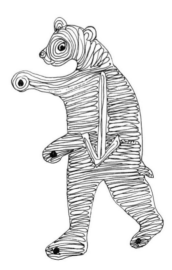

The Search

I search for the bear
claiming his life,
roaming in freedom.
I find his tracks
and step into them
but have not seen or heard . . .

Sudden skyward alert —
A woodpecker chisels time on a tree.

I continue to walk.
Beams of sunlight
wake up the space between trees.
I listen to invisible water flowing.

The bear finds my footprints
and steps into them —
Sets off again from where I started.

Bear Paw Petroglyphs

—Lake Pend Oreille, Idaho—

Before us and before the people called Kalispells,
grizzlies walked trails in one another's tracks.
Hunch-shouldered, they rubbed their backs up
against the same fir's bark spring after spring.
They wore footprints deep into moss.

Crossing in the shallows—
they scuffled stones and loped up across
this ledge of argillite teaching hunters to cross
here, where the rock is red and slick,
glazed first by grinding ice, then ground again
by everyday weather.

Perhaps it was a kind of thanks, this notation,
but someone persisted—took pains to chip
through the patina (color of brick) to heartstone,
blue-gray as ice, below.

They shaped the feet like spear points
pointed backwards—five toes on each,
each toe with a claw. The glyphs
at the margin were made small—
footprints of cubs, perhaps, or children.
The marks through the center of each foot—
seem to be the creases crossing my palms,
the palms of my feet.

purple lupine   (watak.ha)

bear struggles
to dig his way out of the roadside
below shale as brown as his coat

his paws rise slowly up
like the sun

only green as grass

claws distended   purple
as shooting star or pennyroyal root

white tipped as   the mountain
behind the breeze

that celebrates his anger.

The Tale the Bear Left

Its leavings glisten, lump up with tawny rosehip seeds, purple manzanita berries chewed barely and digested less—something of rosehip and berry drawn out, something of bear added back. There is a story here, one written in remains. A creature huge and shambling is tramping the rain-dampened woods of early autumn, a beast of long teeth and heavy fur, hungry for everything, tasting it all. The bear does not live here, on the land I call my own. It wanders through on long loops over canyons and summits, crossing peaks and watersheds, harvesting succulence among pines and firs, trampling over blue lines on plot maps that divide me from the neighbor's logged-over parcel, from the Forest Service's inholding. The bear speaks its truth in eloquent shit: On both sides of the line, this world's small delights taste as sweet.

this poem is for bear

"As for me I am a child of the god of the mountains."

A bear down under the cliff.
She is eating huckleberries.
They are ripe now
Soon it will snow, and she
Or maybe he, will crawl into a hole
And sleep. You can see
Huckleberries in bearshit if you
Look, this time of year
If I sneak up on the bear
It will grunt and run

The others had all gone down
From the blackberry brambles, but one girl
Spilled her basket, and was picking up her
Berries in the dark.
A tall man stood in the shadow, took her arm,
Led her to his home. He was a bear.
In a house under the mountain
She gave birth to slick dark children
With sharp teeth, and lived in the hollow
Mountain many years.
        snare a bear: call him out:
honey-eater
forest apple
light-foot
Old man in the fur coat, Bear! come out!
Die of your own choice!
Grandfather black-food!
        this girl married a bear
Who rules in the mountains, Bear!
        you have eaten many berries
        you have caught many fish
        you have frightened many people

continued on next page

Twelve species north of Mexico
Sucking their paws in the long winter
Tearing the high-strung caches down
Whining, crying, jacking off
(Odysseus was a bear)

Bear-cubs gnawing the soft tits
Teeth gritted, eyes screwed tight
                    but she let them.
Til her brother found the place
Chased her husband up the gorge
Cornered him in the rocks.
Song of the snared bear:
          "Give me my belt.
          "I am near death.
          "I came from the mountain caves
          "At the headwaters,
          "The small streams there
          "Are all dried up.

—I think I'll go hunt bears.
                    "hunt bears?
Why shit Snyder,
You couldn't hit a bear in the ass
                    with a handful of rice!"

Ursa Major

The ice bear traverses the tundra,
a lumbering nomad, fierce
and quick as a lick of cream.
He undulates on invisible bones,
pads plantigrade on soles furred to sculpt the sea,
his coat vanilla and opals and eggshells.
Densely shagged, he shakes off salt
and a circlet of seamoss
then towers, the blue air crackling.
His heart is a flower,
his lungs a map inside his chest.
Black nose visible for six miles,
he scuffles across floes into pockets of snow,
wise to the seamless ice and sky
endlessly acred in blue.

He is the wanderer we would be,
some ancient kin
foraging for steaming seals
great paws baffling the air
scratching his sign in the sky.

The Hunter

This evening I walk across tundra, its long silence
unrolling towards me, plunging in the wind.

In the distance, whiter than bone-dust,
a bear listens to the shape of wind and snow,

smells the far scent of an ivory-toothed whale
gripped in death's tight belly.

It ranges up through ice, through air, to night
where pale dots of light appear beyond the far edge

of a blue frontier, and the moon is a hole
torn at the top of a barren sky.

It is a scene slowly dying until all that remains
is a solitary bear clutching at emptiness;

in a moment the sun too will be gone,
hiding even its sparse embers

as darkness gathers in folds
in a far and quiet recess of winter.

The River

Along this blue porcelain river
wandering like a blind man through a steep valley,
four grizzlies emerge from an orange and yellow forest
chilled by evening and fall's nimble touch.
Slowly, they come downriver
close to the water's edge in search of salmon
stranded upon rock or in shallow eddies;
decaying after summer's long spawn.
From memory I work my rifle's bolt
and lie upon a brittle carpet of fallen leaves
to watch these bears, primitive and instinctual,
and the way their tracks in the sand
recalls the myth of their passing
in these hills where a mottled eagle's shadow
traces an invisible path on autumn's forest floor.
The scent of berries, too ripe and sour,
rises and falls in the slow breeze
that carries my presence, like a beacon,
upriver to the Silverback
rising into crisp air, his large head,
like a metronome, swaying rhythmically
until he finds me in tall grass beneath a treefall.

In an instant they bolt,
not in thunderous clashing, but in silence,
disappearing into darkening trees
until nothing remains but my rapid breathing,
the river, and our footprints pressed into sacred earth.

Sun Bear

I remember you, sun bear,
when I was alone in your equatorial forest,
your dark jungle, hot with monkey urine, mold and swamp.
I bent my legs to a trail and saw the swagger
of you, saw your neck laced in golden fur.

I moved next to mahogany, put my ear to underbrush
and heard you snorting, your tongue lapping termites,
pierced, crushed, struggling.

I stood against mahogany, stood still as sky without clouds.
You trampled around, gnawing sticks, swallowing mosquitoes.
Wind smothered the jungle,
and I knew this was what I'd always wanted – to see

you, your shanks so taut and tar-dark.
You gashed fallen wood with claws sharp as ivory fish hooks,
unaware of me, an animal
smelling of sweat on white hide.

You moved, passed into the dim light
leading my trail and crossed closer.
The earth cracked beneath your bulk
and you lifted your head my way.

Captured by you in this dark canopied cathedral
where death and rain breed life,
we shared the trees, ribbons of sunshine, time.
Together we inhaled,
exhaled,
inhaled like old friends not knowing what to say now

that our moment had come to this unanticipated meeting.
Caught in the confusion
of how I should act
after such a long absence from my own wild body,
you vanished into a river of leaves.
I wanted to chase you.
To this day I don't know how I walked away,
through green walls, without you.

Ursus Redeemed by Darkness

When the first storm unleashes
its white breath, and leaf
by leaf the tree appears to die,
everything conspires to enter
the deep cave of forgetting
and the she-bear lumbers
up the mountain, sighs finally
and rolls on her side. Cubs tumble
in the darkness of her belly,
in a liquid sphere that feeds
on dreams of wild honey, a swarm
of bees, one dark paw dripping.

Under the silent arms of pine,
her lover, the great black bear,
scrapes nuggets of ice from stiff
chest fur. His breath becomes small
clouds in this immediate heaven
and spring is only memory or prophecy,
branches heavy with raspberries, streams
flush with trout. He too will sleep,
fierce ursus, patient keeper of the rope
of stars, who calls the moon
up out of darkness night after night
with his wounded and private desire.

Waking Up Bears

I am the woman who wakes up bears.
I move quietly through the cold,
smile frozen to my teeth,
head encircled by a halo of breath
clinging to my hair.
I pass silently through the stark trees
watching for the next shallow graben.
I've grown very good
at spotting an inhabited cave from far off.

I kneel on the frozen ground and reach in
to plunge my fingers into matted fur.
I feel for the beat of a sleeping heart,
write swiftly to record figures on the charts.
I never tough the cubs.
Even in the depths of this long sleep,
she-bears can wake up fighting,
and cubs won't tell me anything.
They have not suffered yet.

I'm watching for the one
who gave too much,
slept too deeply,
the one whose heart has stopped with cold.
No bears are out tonight.
I am the woman who goes looking for them,
sampling
the metabolism of hunger.

Bear Mother

    Mystery.
Familiarity. Moving together
of bodies. The dance of mouths,
hands, bellies and tongues lightly touching
    knees and hairs and milky toes.

   .   .   .

Black bear mother with magic eyes
and dancing feet
crouching, squatting
giving birth
dropping a single cub
the cub grunting, sticky,
moaning.

Bear

Dropping
only five degrees
Celsius, she enters
that wintry sleep,
her heart
beating a waltz
in slow-
slow time.
She fishes calmly
in that lake of darkness,
dreaming of salmon,
steelhead, crowberries,
aspen-catkins,
molasses, bacon grease,
and the warm
metallic taste
of blood.
Having sidestepped
privation,
having refused
to piece out comfort,
she wakes again in April
to forage the frontier
of life and death
full of a nonchalant
and hungry joy.

The Bear Emerges

The sky shudders with first
thunder of the spring. Bears
shake themselves and rise
to the voices above
and together, bears and sky
make a new year begin.

In bed we hear the rumble,
distant, as we find again
under blankets and our skins,
the deep-set thud of heartbeats.
All through the hard winter
we forgot about rain and lightning.
We were alone except for
a cardinal and a pine. Now

as the day comes to life
we think of bears awakened
to sky-drums and wild onions.
We think of their growls
and claws scraped over bark.
We open a window: wet air
breathes into the house. Again
we are alive, again we are all alive.

As If

A bristlecone – spidery as the pines
in old Chinese scrolls –
has rooted itself into the rocks' crevice,
spilling a pool of shade so I can perch here
to wait for the black bear said to roam
after the red syrup
in hummingbird feeders.

I am wishing him here –
up the rocks in his rolling trot,
his fur silky as the musty
blackness last night
outside my window
I stared into so hard
I thought my body would follow my gaze,
floating up and out
and into a bear's world:
shadowed aspen groves
where I could hear a sound like the sea's,
a place where the odor of bear urine
would be a welcome sign
to tell me my clan:
I am wishing him here.

Standing on the shoulders of the scratchy hillside,
we could brood over star-trails,
shuffle our wordlessness
in perfect self-love.
We could sharpen our claws
against the silence
and set out, tree after tree, for the secret hive.
If. As if.
If only.

After his months
under the old snow,

my bear is rising rough-coated, flatfooted,
tottering in the cold cycle
of lull and struggle.
And I am here
caught in my human musk
and history.

An old brown cabin down the road
sports a weather vane I love:
a tin sea churns
as a silver moon drops into it
while an old clipper with white sails
heaves on the roiling water.
The vane swings back and forth,
the ship goes on
flinging its tiny anchor out.

Baby Pink Nose
—Dedicated to the work of my brother John—

Some shoot and skin her,
then sew massive hide to green felt
for a soft and furry black rug,
forever lifeless on the floor of the den.
    You watch her respectfully
    with a smile of pure pleasure
    as she tumbles and spars with her twin.
Some shoot and skin her,
mounting her head with teeth artificially bared
and piercing glass eyes, above the fireplace mantle.
    You chuckle at her baby pink nose
    as she scurries up a tree
    and peeks out from the backside.
Some shoot and skin her,
because it is black bear season
and licenses are still issued
despite clear decline in numbers.
    You track her quietly
    for a research project,
    noting location of her den,
    the numbers and health of cubs.
Some hungrily watch her
through crosshairs of the rifle
or rangefinder of the bow,
hands damp, hearts pounding with adrenaline.
    From atop a nearby rock
    through the lens of your camera,
    you watch her forage and nurse young.
    Your hands steady, at peace; your heart full.
Some proudly tie her still warm, majestic body
across the hood of a four wheel drive vehicle,
a thin trickle of her lifeblood
slowly making its way back to the earth.

You carefully sedate her,
gently take measurements of teeth and paws;
her health and vitality concern you.

. . .

Perhaps there is a middle ground,
but if so, no one yet knows.
And still in every rug and trophy,
there once was a baby pink nose.

Elegy for a Bear

Sky collides with shadowy clouds
wind and rain come simultaneously.
Pale light falls from the moon
in the squint narrow cave.

Wind and rain come simultaneously,
the forest melts into shadow.
In the squint narrow cave
cubs squeal for milk.

The forest melts into shadow,
a blood-filled mother heaves,
cubs squeal for milk,
crawling onto her cooling body.

A blood-filled mother heaves,
bullets glint in her eyes.
Crawling onto her cooling body,
the cubs begin to starve.

Bullets glint in her eyes,
pale light falls from the moon.
The cubs begin to starve,
sky collides with shadowy clouds.

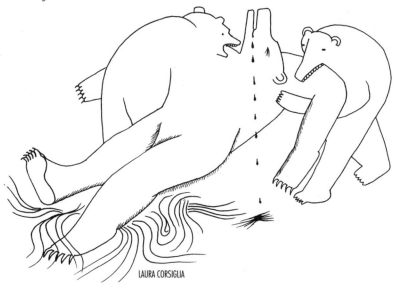

LAURA CORSIGLIA

The Bear

What ruse of vision,
escarping the wall of leaves,
   rending incision
into countless surfaces,

   would cull and color
his somnolence, whose old age
   has outworn valor,
all but the fact of courage?

Seen, he does not come,
move, but seems forever there,
   dimensionless, dumb,
in the windless noon's hot glare.

More scarred than others
these years since the trap maimed him,
   pain slants his withers,
drawing up the crooked limb.

Then he is gone, whole,
without urgency, from sight,
   as buzzards control,
imperceptibly, their flight.

Last Bear Poem
— The Old Marquette Inn

She-bear, Kodiak, color of honey,
of straw, blazing
against oak ceiling and wall,
rears up next to the elevator, rises
to chandelier, to marble and brick.

       Sleepwalker, hands outstretched.
       Old denner, wanderer of woods,
       browser of bush:

Head thrown back. Teeth bared:
Rough pad of palm,
hook and razor of claw.

       Berry-gorger, insect-hunter, lover
       of clover and bees.
       Tree-climber, flower-dreamer:

Light catches her now in a halo.
Now the belly, the mane hair
draping from hip, from thigh.

       Fisher, swimmer under the surface.
       Sad dancer, big humpback,
       snoozer through winter and snow:

Did she bellow? Did the earth
shake when she fell?
He must have stroked her forehead, must have
run his fingertips over her burnished shoulder.
Did he kneel then? Did he lie down
along her warmth, inside her golden arms?

Sleep Now,
His Long Breath Is At Your Shoulder

THE HUNGRY BEARS chased the poor Indian girl. When they almost had her, she turned into a feather and floated away out of their reach. Then, while she was a feather in the air, the girl turned into a long sewing needle and she pierced the bears in the heart, killing them. Then she turned back into a person again.

—from an Ahtna myth

Crazy Jane Meets a Bear

"I've been looking for you everywhere,"
she says when she finally meets him.
She has been chasing the bear, but the bear
is smart. He kneels down
to brush over his tracks with the soft
branch of a fir. He catches a hint
of her scent, and is gone. It's not
that he's afraid of Jane, he just
doesn't want to meet her by himself
in the woods. Everyone knows
how crazy she is. No one knows
what she might do, if provoked. She
has no fear of bears. She's always wanted
a dance partner taller than herself.
Sometimes she carries a bag of berries,
a slab of ham, to attract the bear,
preferably a grizzly. If she's going
to go to all this trouble, she wants
to find a big one. She knows
he could rip her apart with those strong
hands, knows he could lift and toss her
out of his path, but she's used
to the risk. She muses
to herself, "Can a girl propose?"
She decides not to stand
upon etiquette. He is afraid
she would embarrass him
if he introduced her
to his friends. She never did
have much fashion sense. "I am
divorcing my husband and moving in
with a bear," she announces
at a party. Then she plunges her hand
into a pot of honey. "Some sweets
I reserve for him," she says, licking
her own fingers.

Dreaming Bear

The entire bear fits in her palm,
silver makes the animal shiny and safe.
A life line of turquoise and sugilite streaks
its body, imbeds a shadow.
Your body I held whole last night.
How lovers become containers
withholding flesh from extinction
for another turn of the moon.

The bear's legs almost touch,
hollowness creates a keyhole,
we lose ourselves in this thin-aired place
where stories do not overlap. The bear can not
breathe deeply. We consider leaving,
but a shared dream warns: the only exit a mouth
and the hand raw and ready suffocates.
Wait. Rest. Some kindness will stir.

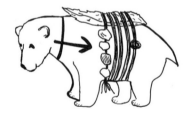

Sleep Warm

Tatshenshini River

Sit by the river
he watches from the willows

Travel summer's spruces
he walks just out of sight

In meadows swept with flowers
he noses your track

Through the first snow
he paces before you

Heavy shoulders
dark arms

Sleep now
his long breath is at your shoulder

Bears at Raspberry Time

Fear. Three bears
are not fear, mother
and cubs come berrying
in our neighborhood

like any other family.
I want to see them, or any
distraction. Flashlight
poking across the brook

into briary darkness,
but they have gone,
noisily. I go to bed.
Fear. Unwritten books

already titled. Some
idiot will shoot the bears
soon, it always happens,
they'll be strung up by the paws

in someone's frontyard
maple to be admired and
measured, and I'll be paid
for work yet to be done —

with a broken imagination.
At last I dream. Our
plum tree, little, black,
twisted, gaunt in the

orchard: how for a moment
last spring it flowered
serenely, translucently
before yielding its usual

summer crop of withered
leaves. I waken, late,
go to the window, look
down to the orchard.

Is middle age what makes
even dreams factual?
The plum is serene and
bright in new moonlight,

dressed in silver leaves,
and nearby, in the waste
of rough grass strewn
in moonlight like diamond dust,

what is it?—a dark shape
moves, and then another.
Are they . . . I can't
be sure. The dark house

nuzzles my knee mutely,
pleading for meaty dollars.
Fear. Wouldn't it be great
to write nothing at all

except poems about bears?

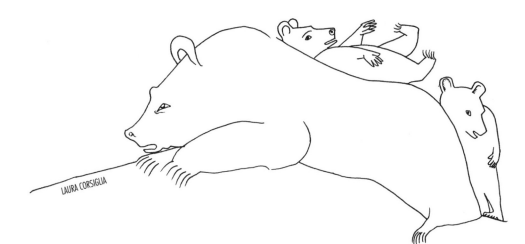

Sleep Now, His Long Breath Is At Your Shoulder

The Brown Bear

The Brown Bear
walked into your bed
lay down with you
threw his right paw
over your sleeping shoulder.

He left before you awoke,
biting off
a part of a claw
leaving it
by your little white feet.

Bear Dance

Like an aphrodisiac the whoosh of highway sound
brings them rushing out:
four brown bears
knocked into my dream by a hit-and-run,

by a streamer of blood Death spun
from a nostril. Tied them up,
held them down on the hot road's shoulder.
I'd have liked to dig my fingers

into your deep brown thatch, bury my nose
in your rich zoo-y soup. I recognize

your daemon as my own,
hidden one, eluder of dreams,
who rears on hind legs like me —

and invite into my life
a bestiary of bears,

quadruplication
of all my fears of death,
the torn fur gouted and mired.

What's a Bear For?
(working with the muse)

In one hand, as if owned, she holds it,
thinking this is what she has ripped
from my flesh: a clean long piece of sinew
she now wants to give back to me.

And bear arrives with an embrace that holds
all fur and deep earth around my ears. Walk softly,
I tell myself, and don't take up too much room.
Claws, five inches long, will rake the bark of a tree,
turn over rocks along the trail, and tear my flesh
from bone. Bear awakens my warm breath, flows the blood
faster from my heart. The wind tells my presence
to any dog's nose, and ears will listen.
The bear is not a guest invited for dinner
but will lick the platter clean and always search
for more. Bear calls me by name, is the other
self who lives in a cave of long-ago, who lies buried
only to rise when least expected or after a deep
winter's sleep. When I think 'bear' into the night sky
the star is there, helps me to find the way home.

Roll it out, she says, the voice is there.
Fear can be relied upon, even
if it has to be laced together, word
by word, until it roars.

Adumbrations

The brown, humpbacked she-bear who inhabits my dreams,
sometimes lingering after daybreak, a dark presence
at the foot of my bed, defying the dawn,
whose hurricane approach scatters villagers like cardboard dolls,
who came daily one season to the edge of town demanding human flesh
    to forestall her wrath,
she no longer roams the forest where we dwell,
terrorizing my daughter and me,
sending us scrambling – and the child on my back –
up the nearest tall tree or narrow winding staircase,
into the dusty cavern of a windowless attic,
or onto the flat, altiplano roof of our mobile home.

Nor has she remained in the front yard,
where only a month ago she stood in starlight
upright among bracken and everlasting pearl
eating blackberries and bellowing within view of our house,
its large, unblinking sliding-glass windows an invitation
to explore, to dine.
At the glass, hunched and quivering like a mouse, I watched, fascinated.

Yesterday she entered our home –
the front door, torn from its hinges, splintered in the grass –
and sat mindfully on the futon couch, sipping tea.
Can you believe it?
Tea! From a multicolored ceramic mug we purchased at a garage sale,
its lowly social status forever overturned
by anointing with the aromatic oils of this articulate memory.

The bear lingered,
ate a dinner of roast lamb and applesauce,
after which we sipped mulled wine,
sang spirited carols and melancholy ballads,
and, drowsy-eyed, climbed beneath the same thin blanket,
where the broad, deep estuaries of sleep
finally emptied us into the foamy, surf-torn, saltwater day.

The Bear-Spring

When I last dreamed the bear, he rose
from the earth, the trees
parted in his path, twigs snapping, cracking
from his weight, his flesh
swaying as he lumbered up the hill.

When I last dreamed the bear, he climbed
the stairs to my porch, the rough pads
of his feet brushed in whispers
on the wood: my eyes
sliding back into my head when I turned to face him.

When I last dreamed the bear, he laid
his black head on my thigh,
the bear-smell rising rank around us,
his coat bristling my skin,
the great weight of him leaning, leaning into me.

And though we never spoke,
I knew then that he loved me, and so began
to stroke his rough back, to pull him even closer.

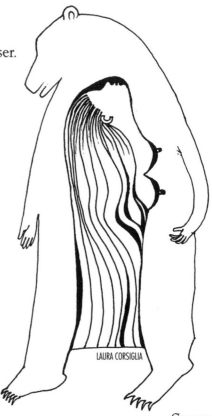

LAURA CORSIGLIA

GRRRRR

Bears

Wonderful bears that walked my room all night,
Where are you gone, your sleek and fairy fur,
Your eyes' veiled imperious light?

Brown bears as rich as mocha or as musk,
White opalescent bears whose fur stood out
Electric in the deepening dusk,

And great black bears who seem more blue than black,
More violet than blue against the dark—
Where are you now? Upon what track

Mutter your muffled paws, that used to tread
So softly, surely, up the creakless stair
While I lay listening in bed?

When did I lose you? whose have you become?
Why do I wait and wait and never hear
Your thick nocturnal pacing in my room?
My bears, who keeps you now, in pride and fear?

Letter to Beowulf

Sleeping under that bear tree the other night
at Young Lakes in Yosemite, I thought of you,
Beowulf, laying down your sweet head in Heorot.

We had hung two packs of food from a stout limb,
then discovered claw marks raking up the bark
of the lodgepole, high into broken branches –

and just at the roots a pile of fresh bear scat.
Well, no one's ever accused me of being a perfect
Boy Scout, much less a Nordic warrior, but like you

I bridle at the name of coward. So I made my boast,
"Here I lie, I can do no other," and took up my abode
for the night. How stupid we were, Beowulf,

how oafishly arrogant to wait on our backs
for the monster. You chose to put aside all arms,
but I gathered a pile of stones on either side

of my sleeping bag, not to mention a flashlight
(the Wonderbright) and a plastic whistle
(the Thunderer) ready at hand. And when he came –

ah, when he came – past dead of night, I fetched
my glasses from my boot and found them fully
fogged with dew. I heard a scratching, sprayed

my light, and lay back down unsure who had prevailed –
or if the bear had come. At dawn I saw our tiny
catchstring pulled up to our drifting packs, but they

still hung undaunted and undamaged there. Granted,
I would like to have torn his shoulder out, and next night
tracked his mother to the bottom of an alpine lake,

but could have been the breeze that blew
our catchstring up, and could have been I trembled
underneath that tree without a cause. That's the price

of being a postmodern hero, Beowulf, a pain I'm sure
you'll never know. Go roast in peace in dragon breath;
we die amid the fumes of our uncertain words.

Winter Bears

In the basement where bears live
is an open river to the north
where we must go.
Bears pace in ovals, rumble
on slickered pads to the rhythm
of wood feathers, seeds that
bloom in quick-step along our path.
We follow the spoor of great elks,
web-hung with mistletoe,
their feet in delicate leaf points;
and badger scat, his wide stripes
furrowed ahead of us, leading north
where we will go, where the lines
line up with white, and 300 words
for snow. The bears stir
in a bear dance of winter coming,
they trek for caves where seasons slow
and the woofle of deep reversible sleep
keeps time with chains of inner earth.
There in the north, the wise one
holds aloft her icicled fingers,
five-sided paw prints to mark a borealis
and the bears, rustling fur to fur,
wend steadfastly up the map, counting
the latitudes of their going.
I puff out my breath, harmonic to their throaty
g r r r r r
As we go they tell me of last April
when they woke to blazed greening
and air charged with equinox.
How they paused at the cave to gather
their heart beats, sleek their coats,
with a dreadful emptiness insistent on forage.
They had slept all those white months
in the haunches of the wise one.
Again we move toward that pool
of charmed bear, compelled by sleep
and the lowering of heads, fur-curled
together in dens of this season.

Legs, the broad ridges of backs,
thick necks, their ears round as clam shells
cocked for winds from the north
and their nostrils bold.
I would crawl into their furnaces,
slip among cilia to the brain of bear
to curl in their secrets
and leach out their myths,
so by this thirst I could become them,
bears heading north where the cave
haunts each season, sinking its message
into berry and fish that the curve of claw
has enfolded this year, pulling out
the long string of winter to come
and the bears unblinking, my two-legged stride,
my furless parchment naked and chilled.
Their great neck humps shake down
the long spines of musked pelt;
shift a little to load me in
to the center of their navigation where I breathe
the cumulus of brown fur, prickling my cheeks
as we match strides, ever north
toward the white horses — toward
a cave where we'll rest in a circle,
these bears holding back their teeth.
Their claws click on granite and dried oak leaves,
on a path no one sees, on the path pulling north
toward the end of the day, toward a cave
full of fur clumps and powdery lost bones
where the dust floor has hollows
that call to night-bears who are weary
of trails and ready to slumber,
their dreams on their shoulders.
We have followed the scent lines, heard
the crow rasp overhead, smells of autumn
are behind us decaying into spring
and the hoary dried smell of ice hangs low,
still pulling us toward that high shelf
where nightmares linger
and the stars are curtained.

My Friend the Bear

Down in the bone myth of the cellar
of this farmhouse, behind the empty fruit jars
the whole wall swings open to the room
where I keep the bear. There's a tunnel
to the outside on the far wall that emerges
in the lilac grove in the backyard
but she rarely uses it, knowing there's no room
around here for a freewheeling bear.
She's not a dainty eater so once a day
I shovel shit while she lopes in playful circles.
Privately she likes religion – from the bedroom
I hear her incantatory moans and howls
below me – and April 23rd, when I open
the car trunk and whistle at midnight
and she shoots up the tunnel, almost airborne
when she meets the night. We head north
and her growls are less friendly as she scents
the forest-above-the-road smell. I release
her where I found her as an orphan three
years ago, bawling against the dead carcass
of her mother. I let her go at the head
of the gully leading down to the swamp,
jumping free of her snarls and roars.
But each October 9th, one day before bear season
she reappears at the cabin frightening
the bird dogs. We embrace ear to ear,
her huge head on my shoulder,
her breathing like god's.

Song Beginning in Big Sleep

The poet loves the bear who sleeps
such a long time in his skin. The bear
might stand like a man, eat like a man,

but it's the big sleep that makes the poet
fall in love with the bear's going still
while his world disappears under snow.

So each spring, when the river runs
and the bear shakes off the last of
sleep like drops of water caught in fur,

the poet dreams of winter. First the pines
stiffen in wind. Then crows start to streak
across the snow, the river runs colder,

the bear sleeps. If the poet could get close
without rousing the bear, she would hear
a sound like fur stirred by wind. But the bear

keeps hidden, sleeping to live. Or it will keep
hidden, when winter comes—it's still spring,
remember, and the poet's only dreaming

of winter, learning to let go of every desire
but finding the way from river to meadow,
past the last asters to the heaved granite.

The only thing she can take to the cave
is willingness to sleep. Will it be enough?
She lies still remembering that some bears

peel grapes with nothing but their teeth.
The poet thinks of the song this would make.
A close-up song, like blood on bone.

Thin, so thin the wind might never pick it up.

She will have to do it, then . . .

Winter Sleep

If I could I would
Go down to winter with the drowsy she-bear,
Crawl with her under the hillside
And lie with her, cradled. Like two souls
In a patchwork bed —
Two old sisters familiar to each other
As cups in a cupboard —
We would burrow into the yellow leaves
To shut out the sounds of the winter wind.

Deep in that place, among the roots
Of sumac, oak, and wintergreen,
We would remember the freedoms of summer,
And we would begin to breathe together —
Hesitant as singers in the wings —
A shy music,
Oh! a very soft song.

While pines cracked in the snow above,
And seeds froze in the ground, and rivers carried
A dark roof in their many blue arms,
We would sleep and dream.
We would wake and tell
How we longed for the spring.
Smiles on our faces, limbs around each other,
We would turn and turn
Until we heard our lips in unison sighing

The family name.

Bear With Me

The notoriously weak eyesight of bears
May account for why they stalk me in dreams:
As threes and safe teddies and cave dwellers,
As mountain ramblers and fishers of streams.
They convene in my backyard late at night,
And while I attempt to sleep into peace,
Shuffle toward my backdoors without fright.
The cute cubs' sizes then seem to increase
As the darkness grows darker in my room.
Brute black shadows prowl closer—with roars!
Approaching my lair, they rear back and loom,
Loathsome snouts callous, and pressure my doors.
Now no efforts can keep them from coming.
They crowd in slowly, crushing my backdoors,
And before me they're swaying and snuffling.
All then shamble across my creaking floors,
And stand upright to see even better.
Just barely seen, they reek of bear rankness,
The heavy essence of rancid butter.
Awakening under the weight of this stress,
From hibernation I rise on all fours,
Morning eyes weak and unable to see.
Once upright, I see the unlockable doors
Between the bears and the bareness of me.

How to Trap a Bear

In the mountains it is easy.
He'll know you as a motion.
You'll know him as
a black-brown wall of fear
blocking the sky.
Kuma means bear
and *kumo* means cloud
both appear suddenly
and change everything.
Climbing in the mud
far away from the warm city
where we met
easy to forget the thatched-roof
Tokyo restaurant with
cold sake in clay pitchers,
wood-beam mandala ceilings
and greetings scribbled
by famous guests like Octavio Paz.

You were cook and bear hunter,
selling his meat to country *ryokan*
keeping his fur to trade for fuel.
I followed you up a mountain
named Horse's Saddle for its curves
you let out a wild yawp
stripped down to nothing
wore only a bear skin,
kept a claw for a souvenir
around your slender neck,
dreamt aphrosiac dreams
and rolled on the mountain floor
absorbing his scent.

You sang an aria
as I watched my
former self fall a hundred feet
and die on the rocks below.
My knees shook when I looked down

and I couldn't move.
When you walked away, one by one,
"unable to watch me die"
I reached out for
the branch I couldn't see,
reached into nothingness
to pull me over to the other side.
I closed my eyes and imagined:
who or what would be there if I made it?
That's when I found that claw-footed
sniffer of all that is sweet and alive
rushing with blood and true
in me.

You found wild *shiitake* and mountain fern
to cook with *soba* noodles
over the campfire.
It was my last meal as a follower
and one of the best meals
I have ever eaten.

You taught me how to trap a bear.
Throw your neck back.
Wear a fish around it.
Put a honey-covered apple
where you want him.
Climb a wild mountain in the spring
learn to speak in grunts
see everything before it sees you
be a poet
and tell no one.

For a long time I couldn't forgive you
for precisely what set me free
but now
my season of hibernation is over,
and the bear
remains free
at the summit,
unchained.

East Moriches, NY

Bobbing on the surface: a stuffed bear, a knapsack
filled with frozen steak, a photo of a black dog.
They tell the divers not to look at
faces, because faces personalize death.

On the list, I see my sister's name. But it wasn't
my sister. Someone else with her name
caught that flight. Still, in a moment of parallel time,
between takes in a movie, my sister stands
with me watching a tame bear. The bear has mitts
on his paws so he won't scratch the floor.
He slips and falls, and the filmmakers laugh,
complain he's so tame he has no charisma.

That bear, they insist, wouldn't hurt anyone.
But while I'm watching them, the bear eats my sister.
Then they feed him morsels of meat
from a dank knapsack and say, "Good boy."

Reason in Its Dreams

The bear is above me.
I feel his breath on exposed skin.
I think of nothing as he gently puts his open mouth round
That thin trunk of my neck.
The huge teeth like tusks crush bone.
A wooden model, a skeleton.
Toothpick ribs of an extinct creature.
The amazing number of delicate bones,
The neck splinters.

This should not be my dream
I suffered through it waking too late.
The pitch of night
I had not survived..
The dream truly belongs to my husband.
He is the one who dreams of hostile bears.
I am the one who most fears man.
He is forever running running in his sleep.
Taking with him the sheets and my repose.
He always wakes before being caught.
Wakened by his panting cry for help, I express sympathy, compassion.

I am furious at having to die from the trauma of a dream created by another.
I cannot accept the speed, the finality of this ending.
A death of such magnitude, the borrowed image.

how the bear came to me

Years ago a lover dreamed I came back from the airport unexpectedly,
crawled into bed in the early morning to surprise him.
When he turned to hug me,
I was a huge black bear.

In honor of his dream I bought a silver bear pendant,
bear earrings followed, bears at my throat.
His dream became mine.
On the phone I growled fierce or friendly.
As a bear, I listened
to bird songs, ate flowers, swam,
fished, decorated the walls with magazine pictures
I pirated from the tourists, took dream journeys.

If you must know, I have
a better sense of humor as a bear.

If I agree with you,
it is a journey through time,
        don't assume,
I see a straight line of light.

Sometimes I am a woman and sometimes I am a bear.
Sometimes I am the black bear that holds you,
sometimes I am held by a white bear,
his paw mark at the shoulder
blade, faint but undeniable,
even when you tell me I'm dreaming again.

> Did some time with a man who liked coyotes. To me
> he always looked like a lizard.
> I heard a scientist say the reptilian brain thinks
>   fight   or   flight.
>   We fought. We fled.

Alone again.
I am the girl waiting for her first love.
I am the woman waiting for her husband to come back from the wars.

I am the woman who sleeps all night with a white bear,
wrapped in a blanket of thick slick polar fur.

Sometimes when I go upstairs,
there's a black bear and a white bear curled in my bed
like an old Chinese yin-yang swirling into stillness.
Sometimes there's a young black she-bear, a young man.
Sometimes a girl and a white bear.

I try to tell you
                    we are
neither   both   dawn   midnight
alone and beloved
          and you say,
"Don't you have any more of those bear stories?"

Bear

Bear died standing up,
paws on log,
howling. Shot
right through the heart.

The hunter only wanted the head,
the hide. I ate her
so she wouldn't go to waste,
dumped naked in a dump,
skinless, looking like ourselves
if we had been flayed,
red as death.

Now there are bear dreams
again for the bear-eater: O god,
the bears have come down the hill,
bears from everywhere on earth,
all colors, sizes, filtering
out of the woods behind the cabin.

A half-mile up
I plummeted toward the river to die,
pushed there. Then pinions creaked;
I flew downstream until I clutched
a white pine, the mind stepping back
to see half-bird, half-bear,
waking in the tree to wet
fur and feathers.

Hotei and bear
sitting side by side,
disappear into each other.
Who is to say
which of us is one?

We loaded the thousand-pound logs
by hand, the truck swaying.
Paused to caress my friend and helper,

the bear beside me, eye to eye,
breath breathing breath.

And now tonight, a big blue
November moon. Startled to find myself
wandering the edge of a foggy
tamarack marsh, scenting the cold
wet air, delicious in the moonglow.
Scratched against swart hemlock,
an itch to give it all up, shuffling
empty-bellied toward home, the yellow
square of cabin light between trees,
the human shape of yellow light,
to turn around,
to give up again this human shape.

The Heavy Bear Who Goes With Me

"the withness of the body"

The heavy bear who goes with me,
A manifold honey to smear his face,
Clumsy and lumbering here and there,
The central ton of every place,
The hungry beating brutish one
In love with candy, anger, and sleep,
Crazy factotum, dishevelling all,
Climbs the building, kicks the football,
Boxes his brother in the hate-ridden city.

Breathing at my side, that heavy animal,
That heavy bear who sleeps with me,
Howls in his sleep for a world of sugar,
A sweetness intimate as the water's clasp,
Howls in his sleep because the tight-rope
Trembles and shows the darkness beneath.
— The strutting show-off is terrified,
Dressed in his dress-suit, bulging his pants,
Trembles to think that his quivering meat
Must finally wince to nothing at all.

That inescapable animal walks with me,
Has followed me since the black womb held,
Moves where I move, distorting my gesture,
A caricature, a swollen shadow,
A stupid clown of the spirit's motive,
Perplexes and affronts with his own darkness,
The secret life of belly and bone,
Opaque, too near, my private, yet unknown,
Stretches to embrace the very dear
With whom I would walk without him near,
Touches her grossly, although a word
Would bare my heart and make me clear,
Stumbles, flounders, and strives to be fed
Dragging me with him in his mouthing care,
Amid the hundred million of his kind,
The scrimmage of appetite everywhere.

The Bear

Not first of my choices
is the Bear—
to be, for example, a bear.

Unlike the Panther
whose taut fur worships
all that is panther,
the least inflexion of his black
one-minded will,

the Bear wears
someone else's clothes,
his lardy haunches
moving like afterthoughts.

Among the killers, he is an oaf.

See how, leaving the air
for barely breathing,
his sleep dismisses him.

And when, out of his snow-
dulled dream,
his stomach stirs him to a lust,
he turns to berry buds,
gorging his great gut
in the prissy kitchens of the birds;

continued on next page

or, mindless of his own malaise,
he raids the bees' sweet siloes,
sucking his guilty fingers like a child.

No, not the Bear,
not this lumbering hunk,
this thud-footed,
sotty-eyed, butt-
heavy burglar,
snatcher of spent salmon,
licker of abandoned bones —
No, never the Bear!

But somewhere I seem
to remember a bear in a cage —
a bear in a small untended cage;
remember turning back,
despite the steam of feces and pee,
to a compelling hurt:

There in the deepest
tunnels of his eyes, he fixed
Me with his memory —

the great sleeves of his knees
remembering rock and bark;
his shawled paws twitching
invisible fish.
          And deep
in the suck of that primitive pain,

against a reredos of pines,
the quiet ministrations of a stream,

I fattened like a buddha
in the sun.

All That Is Left Is To Name Him

AFTER KILLING the two women her husband had left her for, Arnarr turned into a giant bear and attacked her unfaithful husband, ripping him into pieces! Then, still as the bear, she returned to her village and killed everyone there. Afterwards, she roamed the tundra for years until the day hunters killed her. "When they skinned the great bear, they found a dead woman inside. They knew then that the bear was Arnarr.

—from a Central Yupik myth

The Philosophy Professor Discusses
the Nature of the Self-Conscious Mind
(or The Invisible Bear)

"Please do not think about bears," he says
and try as I might, here he comes, big and white,
loose jointed, lumbering over the ice flow of the page.

"And please do not consider your Social Security number
and how you are dressed at the moment," and those things,
too, come to rest beside the bear who is now sprawled

casually in the middle of the floor like a family pet,
becoming more and more familiar in all of the places
that he should not be; so I put on my coat

to cover the clothes that I am not wearing
and add my phone number to the list of trivia
that I am supposed to suppress, and try not to remember

the biologist who once explained that an invisible
object, like a polar bear, can appear white, and suddenly
I am snow-blind in Ohio. Now the bear tilts his head,

confidently, as if he knows the answer to some question,
and now he has forgotten the answer and is content
to snuzzle between the pads of one fat paw.

Already I can smell the pungency of wet fur,
can feel his cold nose in my ear, and I know for a fact
that Kant, Kierkegaard, and Sartre all owned bears,

big, fat, slumbering creatures whose paws twitched
in their sleep as they contemplated essence versus
existence among polar seals, and in my mind

I have already accepted him as a plush reality,
have already bought him a bed, checked his teeth,
paid the vet. All that is left is to name him.

Pigbear

Pigbear could not
live anywhere let alone
in a cave somewhere
out in the wild forest
surrounded by earnest
birds dedicated to
generations.
Their delicate
perorations upon
self-sufficiency
abraded Pigbear
mercilessly; there is
not charity between feather
and fur.
The only place
Pigbear felt safe
was under tables
surrounded by knees
and ankles. When people
bumped against his stubble
they thought it was only
their dog. You might
wonder what Pigbear did for
dignity. He did without dignity.
He said it was hard enough to
live simply.

The Beginning

Until
rising more slowly
    than he has ever risen, he shuffles toward the door
      his ponderous effort to be quiet is futile
        almost comic
      that he does not wake her
      seems a small miracle
    he is silent only in the moment he turns to consider
      (for the last time, he thinks) the troubled human bed
        but then again, for another moment, when he stops
    to fix the closed door in the eye in his mind
before he turns his eyes, already beginning to dim, to the high moon —
    savagely large, savagely incandescent: *he knows, at last,*
        what home is

      even while he is forgetting
the moment when, had he avoided moonlight,
    had he summoned preternatural will,
he could have shed the few changes and clung to some human form
      but now, plunging through shrubs, through
        the mule-minded tangles of forsythia
    scratching at coarse hair
emergent on his chest, thighs, buttocks,
    back, he determines to *accept,*
to reconcile to this transformation, born again as *bear,*
    monstrously large, monstrously dark
    crashing through backyards and streets
      torn by thickets
to find a place where the night is manifestly black
      he knows what home is:
    looks back only once
      through the swath in the bushes
to the door and beyond where love droned
    murmured, sang songs of the small
   human heart, he tilts back his broad head
and lifts flared nostrils to the particles of her scent
    still redolent in the cold air

continued on next page

and smells fear, his own fear, senses the need for stealth
becomes aware that he *senses* this
and thus muses (he says to himself—*muses*)
on whether this is the beginning
of the wisdom of dark woods
or the fading reason of a *man* who knows the dangers
for a beast in this town near the city
who knows, at last, what home is

but not where.

He must think carefully
he thinks.
He recalls a small cool room with one window
that looks to the sun as it rises
a room, cave-like in its clarity, the cave that is home
hidden near a stream
where fat fish, in exuberant moonlight, glimmer in the colors of jewels:
that will be home once he has attended
to invention
learned the craft of killing for sustenance;
taken heed of those who came before,
their alchemy
that turns stones to ripe berries, heavy with juice
and the color of blood.

He knows *where* home is. There is no turning back
as there may have been once
at the appearance of signs
which he ignored too long

signifying changes of the kind he had become accustomed to ignoring.
When he acknowledged them
at last
he thought of age—
a proliferation of hair on his back,
dimming sight, clumsiness,
other signs that he was not exempt, as he had believed, from decline.
Tonight, too, he stayed too long,
not leaving enough time

before he will face the intrusive day
delayed but briefly by the metallic indifference of dawn
Mother Darkness will offer him to it—her necessary oblation—
with only the grimmest avenue of reprieve.

The trees are black, flayed by autumn to their skeletal form
black against savage moonlight.
He moves toward the light (always
toward the light)
and lifting his nostrils into the air again, he smells blood
from the torn meat of his haunches
tastes metal in his mouth, feels emptiness
at the center, names hunger, thirst, pain, fear
pauses to focus
and turns, in time, to imperatives:
keep moving
find food, water
shelter,
rest hidden throughout the day
wait for darkness
begin to move again
dodging the machines of men
their beasts
find open light   find open light

light made unspeakably clear, unspeakably beautiful
by the coat of wild darkness it wears.

Bear Warning

In the sand along the lake
someone's footprints splay
sand bearlike. Or a
bear has snuck among
us, disguised as a rational
being, and we have not distinguished
his growls in the morning
from ours. We're all heavy
and hairy this year. And
snort, snuffle, swing our arms
as we walk upright, and
remain mute and yellow-eyed
when accused of tracking
mud across the floor.

LAURA CORSIGLIA

Bear Song

If I were a bear
with a bear sort of belly
that made it hard to get up
after sitting,
and if I had paws
with pads on the ends,
and a sort of a tab
where a tail might begin,
and a button eye
on each side of my nose,
I'd button the flap
of the forest closed.

And when you came
with your wolf and your stick
to the place that once was
the place to get in,
you'd simply be
at the edge of the town,
and your wolf wouldn't know
a bear was around.

Outside Pagosa Springs

1.
It was the bear with her talent
For slow grazing that hit against
My daughter's car, Red Subaru
With the Pleiades on the hood.
The young female bear
Lumbered out of dark
Into a beam of light and back
Into dark again. The bullet
From the State Police stanched
Her pain. It was my daughter
Driving north for love. In our
Family we always head that way—
Into the bear, due north, in fur.
It was the thud of bear my girl
Age twenty knew. Same year
She stopped eating meat, her
Senses grew too keen. She bought
Cranberries, rose hips, honey
At the store. The light grew strange
And thin on her. When she was young,
Her beastly beauty proved too much
For me, I wished for ancient Greece
Where they'd take the young girls off
And dress them in a robe made
Of bear. A pelt to obscure
What men might see too soon and want,
Trained to grow their minds first.
The bear gave my girl a claw to tear beneath
The surface. Remember Red Rose's groom
Snagged to gold on the threshold?
This drift of the natural against her car
Gave her an entry to the other land
Where tombs shine with fruit and flower.
Where babies' heads crown between
Animal legs. This bear came slowly for sacrifice
And so made holier the daughter I love
More than I love woods and words. Gave

Sacred to sacred. So I offer thanks.
It was as if I came out of the woods
To wake her with my great dull hand.

2.
Moving toward what I sensed, with my
Fourth dimensional eye and ear,
My snout for rooting out beauty.
Like a bright berry in summer, though
It was dark. I could hear it coming.
Berry through the night, great circles
Of beauty and feast aimed at me.
And I left my mother's cave and my
Father's cave, for I was a bear
Grown to learn and I leathered
My way through trees to what
Was calling me. Like water
In a river the lights streamed.
I went to drink, thirsty and the light
Smelled good. Keen to drink everything
On earth. The berry came quickly huge
And I met it with my head and mouth,
My paws in the air, I flew. The river
Slipped me back and we both stalled.
Such stillness, the engine of the night
Beat in me. I was a bear receiving grace.
Gratitude to my ancestral tombs.
I was in the grail, ancient blood draining
The sound out of me. A human like
A white berry cried. I smelled
Fear and love. I'd never smelled
Love before in human form. Oh,
I'd known the rough jaw of my mother.,
But human love came like a quail.
Something small and quick
Following its own kind. I inhaled
So I could make it last. I couldn't run
So I took to heart what metal sacrament
I had to take. Then I flew. Fled that smell
And river. Rose like Russian dancing bear.

continued on next page

Higher still, saw that scene below
Smelling of tarmac and Ponderosa Pine.
Rising over a well lit clump of humankind,
I donated my beauty to this girl. Sacrificed
My nudity and fur. I gave and gave
As the bullet fit my heart's cave.
I was the bear and now she bore
My weight in her too small body
And I saw that she, of all of them,
Was one who understood and could.

Ursa Minor

Sometimes my sister is bear/woman,
great shambling beast intermittently
emerging ill-tempered from a darkened den,
ravenous, plumping her flesh with pot
roast, half a pie, heaps of bean salad,
mugs of coffee, liters of Coke.

The house holds its breath, awaits her temper—
scimitar words clawing open the unarmored
breast, dull resentment smoldering
silently behind narrowed eyes, or,
appetite appeased, bulky body
dragging back to hibernate.

Sometimes she tries to socialize,
smearing lipstick greasy bright,
scattering awkward smiles, circus bear
dancing muzzled for the ignorant,
swaying its great shining head.

Self-Portrait

I move about inside thick bear skin fur.
The image in the mirror is that of a woman.
It is the correct mirror for others.
They suspect fur, but seeing only
skin, brush away the impulse.

All the springs of my life,
I've tried shedding this fur,
but bone knowledge has eluded me.
I am left with only an outline of myself,
confusing the cave for the jeweled inner realm,
a black expanse around my questions.

This year I move towards knowing,
carving my steps along the spring thaws,
running the length of the dark, wintered psyche.
In the snow beside me appears Auntie,
that mystic forebear of women,
hunched in the direction north.
We run on a path of divided urgency:
one trail the sinewy, painful footprints of history,
the other, unlit, containing the resilient spirit
that waits alone, fed by the discards of poets
and the shiny remains of a moon.
In her light, Auntie's dappled shape is reflected;
these two guardians of wisdom race ahead of me.
I follow, slower, on two legs, younger,
of short history, lumbering toward home.

Was a Bear

Loved honey,
salmon & sleep.

Was a bear during winter
alone in the den.

Was a bear, my mother
growling in a den.

Was a bear jumping hoops
on fire & asleep.

The bear like most bears
loved her honey & cubs.

Is a bear now so old
padding on all 4s.

Is a bear in a den
growling at herself.

Is a bear, what's a bear
doing in bed, refusing

her porridge, STUFFED!
Shaking her head.

Is a bear over there
in that chair wheeling circles

back to cubness (but
threadbare, all gristle, though

was a bear, is a bear, always a bear.)

White on White

My fur rushes
like cold water under thick ice,
and in a snowstorm,
my giant girth
  all but disappears.

Now civilized, hot days carry
bus loads of women who compare me
to the color of cream or
  lightly-baked custard.
They snap tiny pictures
  with tiny cameras,
  where I look like
  a tiny thumb print
from their child's
milky hand.

Palest of all my brothers,
with a wilder, more gamey musk
standing straight under my coat
that's difficult to sense at 20 below.

I'm temperately entertaining;
every zoo winter, I always bat snowballs
the youngsters hurl,
high and wide with my paws,
but never did I see snow
like that on the tundra,
a long-running freeze for miles,
or hear wind that howled like wounded wolves
in the ears of my prey,
who never realized
until I struck.

Furry Bear

If I were a bear,
   And a big bear too,
I shouldn't much care
   If it froze or snew;
I shouldn't much mind
   If it snowed or friz—
I'd be all fur-lined
   With a coat like his!

For I'd have fur boots and a brown fur wrap,
And brown fur knickers and a big fur cap.
I'd have a fur muffle-ruff to cover my jaws,
And brown fur mittens on my big brown paws.
With a big brown furry-down up to my head,
I'd sleep all the winter in a big fur bed.

The Day Our Teddy Bears Get Washed

After nights snuggled up
to our sweating bodies,
days dragged around,
then abandoned in a corner,
there comes a day
when they must be washed.
Out in its careful orbit,
Saturn begins to wobble.

i know nothing about bears

except for the white woolly bearskin next to my bare skin and mama singing bye baby bunting so I wouldn't wriggle for the photographer I hugged the skin wouldn't let go and all hell broke loose when she carted me home bearless then later pa said *c'mon for a picnic to city park zoo we'll see the bears too* I sang in the back of pa's pickup all the way and when pa parked I flew out past ma's *don't get lost* heading for the bear cage but where was my white woolly there was nothing but ugly snoutnose in knockkneed lurch just like nathan potato left back in grade one four times who chased me shouting *cockeyed cookie cockeyed cookie* pointing to my wandering left eye until ma's *look at me look straight at me* and I did first with one eye then with the other so they rushed me to the doctor for glasses *no sir no glasses for me* until sister annie said *look you're special second cousin to the ucumari bear in the picture looking smart with glasses just like you* but mr mcpherson the policeman down the block buckled in his bear coat was a different story like a kodiak stomping along scattering kids like marbles scaring us silly until he turned the corner then i'd grab my one-eyed teddy bang his head on the wall just to show who's boss and beg ma to read me pooh bear's adventures climbing trees hunting honey next to pooh i loved the girl next door's toy cub bear you could twist his head right off and see inside a tiny sweet-smelling bottle so i made friends with her played blind man's bluff until she was blind man then i pinched the little bear but ma grabbed me smacked me hard held me upside down and shook until the bottle fell out of my underwear and smashed and everyone said *shame shame* except for uncle faivy a champion hugger stomping in grabbing kids lugging big bakery boxes full of sticky sweet chewy bear claws yelling *come and get it* if you had a loose tooth you didn't need a dentist bear claws did the job much better whenever faivy came he was full of stories about garbage bears finding their way back to camps even though they carted them a hundred miles away my *nix on camping* made the family laugh until the same old arguments began *callisto was a fool to start up with zeus she'd only get in trouble with hera and that sweetheart zeus turned her into a bear got her killed then tossed her up into the sky now she's ursa major some choice* another expert chimed in *don't tell me atalanta was suckled by a bear and paris as well it was shepherds who found and took care of him besides the midrash says bears lack mother's milk* meanwhile the totem maven droned on about *the heavenly origins of bear the son of god descending from heaven and back up when he died* then babbled on about karelia bear ceremonies and the nasty story about a woman fucked by a bear giving birth to a finnish tribe until everyone shouted *enough you've killed our appetites* while i years from all that kitchen talk hibernate in cave of night and follow tracks you plow but your dark animal in its protective coat of sleep prowls away to places i cannot follow until morning when you lift your snout above the sheets growling with hunger and devour me.

Objet d'Art

This small found bear, rescued
from a dumpster, oblivion
of the once-loved, brought
to the studio and wrapped in gauze
from blunt feet to just below
blue plastic eyes, dipped
then dipped again in beeswax
to cover the slip-stitched mouth,
the black felt nose, which hardened
to thick, yellowed skin over
a hand-sized bear, arms and legs
hushed, only the eyes unpossessed –
and in this mute countenance,
a grief so arched in necessity
it has begun to fall away.

Bear

Going down in the elevator
my shiny-haired grandson turned into a bear
pawing the air, growling softly.
I hurried to tell him Momaday's story of *Tsoai-Talee,*
the seven sisters and the brother who chased them,
(*Why?* my grandson asked) becoming a horrible bear,
the girls running to the stump of a great tree
that rose in air. (*Why?*) And they became stars. (*Silence*)

The bear stood up against the tree and lifted
its terrible paws, but it couldn't scare them
any more. The girls were free, "beyond its reach."
And the bear "scored" the Tsoai tree with its claws.

If you go to Oklahoma, where Baba was born,
you will find the stump of the Tsoai tree,
it is deeply grooved. If you look in the sky
even from here, you can see the lights of the Big Dipper,
the seven stars. We crossed Union Square toward Broadway.
My grandson, hand still in mine, waiting for the light
at 16th Street, asked *what happened to the bear?*

How do I know the price of eternal life?

Bears

Remember, we're all bears!
my daughter says. And we are.
Sometimes baby, sometimes sister-bear,
she can change without warning.
But Goldilocks is always the same,
off in another room ruining things —
Mommy-bear! Now Goldilocks broke my other chair!
But I fix it every time — bang! bang!
My carpentry skills are amazing,
and I'm a whiz in the kitchen —
every meal just too hot — so we take a walk
and on return baby-bear's is just right.

If we get there before Goldilocks.
Lately, when she's been around
she sleeps a lot. But we're getting used to it.
Mommy-bear, can we keep her?
We'll roar at her really gently
and she won't be scared.

On the freeway, my daughter asks
if all the people in all these cars are bears.
I pause then say no, I think it's just us.
Silly! Of course they are!
This is bear world, you know!
So as we step out of the car she says,
We're bears . . . be sure to step on all the cracks!
And I do, believing it's our calling.
My big bear feet and her little paws
stomping precisely on every line.

The Black Bear on My Neighbors' Lawn in New Jersey

In my neighbors' front yard where one birch tree casts
its pale shadow over their small, suburban ranch house
and the grass is smooth and freshly mowed,

an enormous black plastic bear stands, its paws
upraised as though ready to attack,
its mouth stretched in a senseless grin.

Every year my neighbors have a garage sale
to get rid of all the knickknacks and fake
country plagues and costume jewelry
and mugs with cutesy sayings on them
that they've accumulated during the year.

Next year maybe they'll try to sell
the ersatz bear with its weird, cockeyed smile
and maybe they'll even find someone like themselves
to buy it, one more accumulation
in a life of acquisitions.

Think of it: this plastic bear
doesn't need the wilderness
to live; it doesn't need food.
Two hundred thousand years from now,
if we let the world survive that long,
the people of the future will find it.
Imagine how confused they'll be
as they try to figure out what use
we could have made of it,
what kind of lives we led.

Not Just Wood

Halloween she wore a witch's hat.
At Christmas, she held a wreath.
In July we tied an apron 'round her,
and leaned up against her feet.

She shielded us from snowballs,
delivered judgments in courts of play,
at night she stood as sentinel
to frighten prowlers away.

As solid as her ancestors,
she weathered every storm.
We expected nothing less
from a bear chainsaw born.

As time goes rolling past us,
situations change a bit:
She doesn't get dressed up much.
We prefer to sit.

Her place is in the den now.
No longer the back yard.
For she's a family member
despite her grooved façade.

The Red and Black

late March, northern Wisconsin

Along Highway 51, where the Bad River
wanders out of earshot, snow pelts my windshield
like huge white diatoms. I make out a roadsign
which says **BEAR HABITAT.** Farther into this sea
of pummeling I sense I must get to the bottom.
Then I hear them calling: *Slow, slow . . .*
turn off into the birches—park your van and leave it . . .
I pull my hands up into my sleeves and listen—
The snow will cover your tracks to our dens—
they cannot follow you. And when it stops you
will have to walk backwards the way you came here.
But how long a song it will be until tomorrow
and what your footprints will resemble is another
story altogether. We are waiting, brother.

It would be fitting, I think, if among the last manmade tracks on earth would be found the huge footprints of the great brown bear.

Earl Fleming

a drum beat,

a heart beat

HAVING TURNED THEMSELVES into giants, Raven and Bear wrestled to see who was strongest. They were taller than fifty trees on top of each other! They pushed and shoved and threw each other down. All the time, they were really kicking up dirt and rocks. When they finished and returned to their true sizes, a mountain stood in the place where they had fought. That mountain is Denali, The Great One.

– from a Dena'ina myth

Shield of the Bear-West

The hide has been stretched round,
    the sacred circle,
        medicine shield of the West,
turquoise inlaid & painted:

above:
    the moon-rise over the sierra,
below:
        the bear stalks;
    he is black, chief spirit keeper.

Round is the shield & blue;
    from it the feathers hang,
        water pennants of the West.

The Bear's Gift

From the Black Adobe Lodge in Wakwaha:
a teaching poem. The meter is nine-syllable,
a meter particularly associated with
Black Adobe verse.

Nobody knows the name of the bear,
not even the bear. Only the ones
who make fires and cry tears know the name
of the bear, that the bear gave to them.
Quail and plumed grass, infant and puma,
all their lives they are wholly alive
and they do not have to say a word.
But those who know the name of the bear
have to go out alone and apart
across hollow places and bridges,
crossing dangerous places;
and they speak. They must speak. They must say
all the words, all the names, having learned
the first name, the bear's name. Inside it
is language. Inside it is music.
We dance to the sound of the bear's name
and it is the hand we take hands with.
We see with the dark eye of that name
what no one else sees: what will happen.
So we fear darkness. So we light fires.
So we cry tears, our rain, the salt rain.
All the deaths, our own and the others,
are not theirs, but our own, the bear's gift,
the dark name that the bear gave away.

Black Bear Dances

Black Bear
        dances
in the shadows
        of the pines
the bones
        of his people

Black bear dances
        with his wounds
with his pain
        he dances
with his rage
        in the
crying rains

His paws
weave symbols
        of his claws
ripped and shining
        in the mist
Black Bear dances
        shaking water
& sweat
        from fur & skin

        Each
paw print
        shows
a people's face
        in red/
dying/
        & by
        white hands
held under
        under the earth
that was once
        sacred
& now is

        a blanket
that holds
        their blood

Where he
        stands
under the
        pale piercing
lighted moon
        the
earth skin
        is mud
Black Bear
        dances
with the light
        streaming
from his eyes

Black Bear
        dances
He dances
        small steps
for woman
        & child
he dances
        sharp small
loops
        for the warriors
Black bear
        dances
in heavy circles
        for the
graveyard
        tribes

Black Bear
        dances
because

        of their
hunger & thirst
        because
something comes
        that is worse
those who
        no longer care
those who have
        lost pieces
of themselves
        to survive
to become white

Yes/
        blood calls
Black Bear
        yes/
        he answers
he dances
        for the ancestors
& those
        who Earth Walk
for all
        who are
of the grave yard
        tribes

Black Bear
        has one
message/
        it is the
end of times
        it is time
to rise
        to rise
to rise/
        Black Bear
        dances

Two Bears

Poor Wolf told how the bear
entered his lodge as he lay
fevered with smallpox. The animal sat,
back to the boy,
thick brown pelt smelling of
humus & pine, scratched
its huge furry breast. "I did not know,"
Poor Wolf said, "if I was dreaming.
The bear left, returned, repeated
the same gesture. When my father came
we talked & agreed, surely the bear
had mercy on me. After that, I worshipped
the bear, & in the dance wore anklets
of bear's teeth."

The boy next door tells of the bear he saw
while grazing channel to channel.
It caught a salmon,
swiping its huge paw into the space between
the beer commercial & the crying family
on *Oprah*. His mother took him to the
Disney Store, bought him a stuffed bear from
Just-So Stories, which sits with the other toys
in his closet.

The Bear That's West in Us

According to some, the awakening of our inner selves is connected to this,
our image of the bear itself,
west on the medicine wheel, a totem of reception and self knowing.
A reminder of how we're all living on some kind of border,

poised between inside and out, sleeping and waking, dreaming or not,

all of us at certain times like them, altering what we know of the physical,
passing into deep sleeps, breathing slowly, the body suspended
and only later, months later in the case of the bear,
come back to a life, berries, honey, a sun's wild message, spring again.

I listen to the wild at night for sounds of bear in the brush,
not the actual bear itself, but always the idea of one,
of a huge brown one, untamed worlds, a raw place, a country of bears
where human plans count less than imagined ones.

A hibernator, bear knows exactly how to wake from the deepest sleep,
knows how to recover,
how to use vehicles of regeneration even scientists can't figure out.

And always they are full of necessary information,
of night's business, old debts, resonators of other means of living,
tracking what's beyond us, out further than we know where to go,
further than I can follow the old brown one even as it leads me on.

To live fully at all may be to dream of the coming of the bears,
a world of life under snow, wintering, loneliness, unexpected turns of fate
before the dazzling effects of change and light and earth in its seasons.

Even now I hear them in the night, the ones that come only in dreams,
some silent, some large, the breadth of the wild near my face,
a taste of it everywhere, old ones, young ones, a world of them, hiding,

rising up in the night, in an endless string of light and shadow,
deep in, deep over, the sleeping bears, all of us in the same world together.

The Bear

1
In late winter
I sometimes glimpse bits of steam
coming up from
some fault in the old snow
and bend close and see it is lung-colored
and put down my nose
and know
the chilly, enduring odor of bear.

2
I take a wolf's rib and whittle
it sharp at both ends
and coil it up
and freeze it in blubber and place it out
on the fairway of the bears.

And when it has vanished
I move out on the bear tracks,
roaming in circles
until I come to the first, tentative, dark
splash on the earth.

And I set out
running, following the splashes
of blood wandering over the world.
At the cut, gashed resting places
I stop and rest,
at the crawl-marks
where he lay out on his belly
to overpass some stretch of bauchy ice
I lie out
dragging myself forward with bear-knives in my fists.

3
On the third day I begin to starve,
at nightfall I bend down as I knew I would
at a turd sopped in blood,

and hesitate, and pick it up,
and thrust it in my mouth, and gnash it down,
and rise
and go on running.

4
On the seventh day,
living by now on bear blood alone,
I can see his upturned carcass far out ahead, a scraggled,
steaming hulk,
the heavy fur riffling in the wind.

I come up to him
and stare at the narrow-spaced, petty eyes,
the dismayed
face laid back on the shoulder, the nostrils
flared, catching
perhaps the first taint of me as he
died.

I hack
a ravine in his thigh, and eat and drink,
and tear him down his whole length
and open him and climb in
and close him up after me, against the wind,
and sleep.

5
And dream
of lumbering flatfooted
over the tundra,
stabbed twice from within,
splattering a trail behind me,
splattering it out no matter which way I lurch,
no matter which parabola of bear-transcendence,
which dance of solitude I attempt,
which gravity-clutched leap,
which trudge, which groan.

continued on next page

6

Until one day I totter and fall –
fall on this
stomach that has tried so hard to keep up,
to digest the blood as it leaked in,
to break up
and digest the bone itself: and now the breeze
blows over me, blows off
the hideous belches of ill-digested bear blood
and rotted stomach
and the ordinary, wretched odor of bear,

blows across
my sore, lolled tongue a song
or screech, until I think I must rise up
and dance. And I lie still.

7

I awaken I think. Marshlights
reappear, geese
come trailing again up the flyway.
In her ravine under old snow the dam-bear
lies, licking
lumps of smeared fur
and drizzly eyes into shapes
with her tongue. And one
hairy-soled trudge stuck out before me,
the next groaned out,
the next,
the next,
the rest of my days I spend
wandering: wondering
what, anyway,
was that sticky infusion, that rank flavor of blood, that
        poetry, by which I lived?

Bear Mother I

(A Haida princess slipped on Bear scat as she was gathering berries, and cursed this sacred animal. Bear came in human form to teach her the meaning of his ancient power. Together, their cubs were the founders of the Bear Clan.)

Oh the odor of her menses,
             rich as huckleberries.
The fruit flesh, ripening her hands.
      The small swelling at the breasts.
Their sweet fullness,
and that lazy careless walk.
        The blood,
            drizzling,
down her slick thighs.

He could smell it a mile away.
His brown fur,
       just slightly,
            raised.
He sniffed himself toward her,
     teeth and gums,
         streaming red.

She should have known.
       Her sisters far ahead.
The faint whistle
    of bear song,
         sailing,
through the air.

      She should have known.
But—he was so fine.
Pelt gleaming,
      the light frost,
          icing
his face.
And those eyes—Bear eyes.
A black stone
     falling,
        smooth
in the river.

continued on next page

She should have known.
But – that brown skin,
                a tender fire.
So fine,
        the salt lick
                of his tongue.
The catch
            of her throat.
The down nestle
            of thigh
                    on thigh.

And when he entered her.
Still, as a winter cave.
        Still, as the tail of breath,
rising.
        A white fog
                between them.
The shape of that other rose.
Their Bear-Child,
                    his coat,
wet and steaming.

And when she opened to him.
        His cum,
tasting,
        of river silt,
                and red fleshed
                        salmon.
The spring thaw rolling down
                    her thighs.
            Loosening her,
the way water,
                loosens
rock.
        Becomes the rock.
                Its mineral body,
the color of blood.

The Bear Sacrifice Ceremony
after Lenape lore and ritual

1
Life begins with woman:

Twenyucis had a dream
before the year's first new moon, at the time of the feast.
"I know where the Bear is sleeping. Call the three young men."

>   We had hiked all day, mid-summer
>   across rocks that sweated, tripped blistered feet—
>   executive, mechanic, bureaucrat-wanna-be poet.
>   Men hot for a little omnivorous stew: instant peas & ham
>   steeped in filtered swamp water. That night

Big Dipper/Sky Bear rose . . .middle night sky
her head upright, three hunters behind.

>   What hollow tree was her home?
>   Where was the boy she had taken?

>   Elsewhere in the city, people killed
>   one another, for the rite of killing one another.

2
>   At dawn we strolled—
>   morning's call of nature—
>   watching, on rumors of you.

Twenyucis said, "Near daybreak you will reach there—
near the creek which runs by, in the elm which leans east.
Look up. There's a hole in the tree—the Bear's home.
From there you cannot leave until you bring her."

>   Didn't the rescued boy say, "She wanted me to stay
>   to join her family but knew the men would come and kill her?"
>   "She said, 'They will raise my cubs.'
>   But she charged them"—

continued on next page

ah, a bear has vulnerabilities –

abrupt anger, powerful & secure: heedless in power
somewhere a man shoots his wife, his children, himself.

3

We made breakfast: coffee on the fire
apple and raisin gruel – the wind carried it
men talking of families

"Then standing up you hit that tree.
With your bow, three times you hit that tree.

You tell the Bear, 'I find you.' Three times
you tell the Bear, 'I find you.'"

At the appointed time
    the Boy-Bear would track, always knew where to find a den.
    But wouldn't kill, wouldn't eat the feast of flesh.
    He would cry, "I caused it. Mother gave me a choice
    to leave or to stay. Staying, I caused it."

        & men talking of war, crows circling overhead:
        "Can you believe we buried Iraqis
        alive in the sand just to see if we could do it?"

"Then you tell the Bear, 'Come down!
Come down, we want your body!
Come and take the lead.'
And the Bear will come with you."

4
Fragment of sky:
        sure-scented, shortsighted bear you came
        into our camp

        we scrambled at the prospect
        of being meat.

"Shoo, bear! Shoo! It is not time for you
to be here!"

The Bear-Boy knew the cycle —

Autumn: three arrows hit his Mother
her head descends, bleeding red on leaves — to fall

prostrate in winter
the white mantle of snow / the ladled grease of her fat.

"She will lead you," Twenyucis said, "back to the people."
"She will give herself for food
so the people can eat the seasons of night."

5
     Bear, after you left, we broke camp
     to return to our cities, what an adventure!
     Discussed this trek again, perhaps

next spring:

when Sky-Bear awakens
head ascending out of her den
   & three hunters trailing behind.

Thunder Swamp, near the Appalachian Trail

In the Sky Are Two Bears

Stars
that trail their blood
over the ice of our eyes.

Their shaggy legs weightless
at winter's end
stumbling

out of the steaming caves of space.

That pair who live by the pattern of their luck
which makes them walk a little drunk
on the wine of dusk

never one without the other
always pursuing.
Always apart.

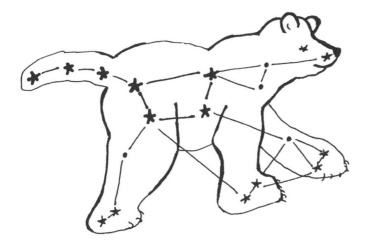

The Burning Bear

How long will the fire leap? How high?
Why ask the wood? You're the woman
who touched its tinder, saw smoke climb.
Flames flung their arms around our bones.

Tonight no moon —
How the Bear glitters!
Each bone a torch
blazing on the border of his life.

Nowhere can this captive Bear escape
his perimeter of pain.
Fire is all we see
of him. Fire is all

the form he feels, his broad limbs glow.
His hide black from haunch to head,
he prowls the snow of stars
until he knows his mate is near —

Flame of her flesh, light of her voice
in the charred sky! His claws curl,
his eyes crack like coal —
He burns, he burns. He will never die.

Playing the Bear

On shards of an ancient vase: girls of ten
running through woods with a bear.
Little Sisters of the Bear, Greeks called them,
sent to the mountains and taught
to know the feral yet contain it, to have

honeysuckle breath, feet that shiver grass
but bruise no blades. To gather fruits,
reel in a meadow of crocus
and asphodel, follow bees to honey,
run with wolf and roe deer.
But as Pan piped of wide-hipped pleasure,
they also learned to be hunted, to
yield wildness yet retain its imprint.

In myths, Atalanta, who was raised
by bears, will marry only the man
who can catch her in a race; and the oracle
tells the childless Kephalos to take
the first female he meets. That female,
a bear, gives birth to a son whom she
suckles reclining as humans do. Then beneath
olive trees, at the darning-needle hum
of midday, she becomes a woman, as do we

under brown hair, under swelling flesh.
Yes, like the girls on the vase we're schooled.
So ring your handbells, offer mead and honey.
But have no fear. Our teeth are
sharp yet careful: they know submission
and how to gentle live flesh.

Family Tree

I picture her, my great-great-great
grandmother, say, in the long arctic summer
dusk where the light, refusing to give over,
keeps on to midnight and beyond. This woman,
bored with husband, farmers, farmers' wives,
bored with gleaming copper and bright aprons,
irritated with the neat parlor freed only
for the prison of the pastor's visit, this woman
longs for darkness. Tonight she's done her chores,
swept the kitchen, prepared the dough, milked
the cows, fed the chickens, hauled the water,
and still the light will not be quiet. So,
she says to herself,

> *Jag tror jag ska gå till skogen*
> I think I'll go into the woods,
> *Kan handa jag möter ett troll,*
> Perhaps I'll meet a troll.

She had heard of women carried off for troll
wives. Even that would be better, to be one
of the queer ones whose eyes never rest
on things but look just beyond, whose hearts
settle at last into real stone instead
of just the pain of stone. So, she takes
off her apron, fixes her hair, and sets
off down a road that dwindles to a trail
that sneaks into a wood.

For awhile she whistles
because boys can whistle but girls must sing, but,
as the trees close over and in, the only
sound she makes is the little catch of breath
that happens at the base of the throat when the heart
beats too quickly. She shivers in her thin summer
dress as the cold lingering close to the ground
from the winter before reaches up to her
and at her. At last the trail runs

continued on next page

out of itself and she stand irresolute,
weight thrusting on one foot then
the other. Should she press forward where
no one has been before? Maybe it was silly,
maybe she should turn around, maybe
there are no trolls.
                              She stands there
deep in wish as will can carry until
a low rumble and she turns to an upswelling
of blackness that rears and spreads its paws so wide
the rank blanket of underfur seems
a door she can enter, a dark door
which closes fiercely around as an immensity gathers
her in against itself.

                              At last,
it drops back to its four paws and lumbers
off impervious to thorn or thicket or the soft
sobbing of my grandmother now just
another hurt girl sitting amidst
the ruin of her clothing able to think
of nothing else to do but go back
home and wait for the year to fall around her.,

            All winter she thickened sleepily in the warm'
cave of her husband's pride in having fathered.
When the lambs dropped in spring, she bore
a lump all suet and hair which she licked
into a human shape. In her aftersleep
she called out – "Bear," and her husband said,
"*Bjorn*. Yes, We'll call him *Bjorn*."

Grandmother

> wakes
in her
> hump-shouldered
smells-bad
stands-like-a-man
shaggy-foot
coat.
> Goes
chuffing through the
honeysuckle.
> Snaps
at a butterfly.
Shits.
Slaps
> dandelions.
Scratches
> her
cranky
old
ass on a tree.

Toward Morning the Inuit Grandmother Talks to Herself

Today I go with the Bear who comes in my dreams.
I have softened too many skins with my teeth
and the animals want me. My fingers are the bones
of my needles. Snow cries in the spring,
nobody likes to leave, my father told me.
We are here, we go other places, we make room
for the children. My son's wife is moving
under her blanket, my body takes no heat
from the ashes. I have been cold before.
The Bear outside, I hear him, it is time.
There is not much he will have. It is time.

(After a story by Robert Coles)

Relic

We keep the finger-bones of saints
in holy shrines, yellowed joints
laid out on purple velvet.
And the faithful come,
pressing their foreheads
against the glass case,
breath after breath fogging
the mirror of their prayers.

So how will we worship the thigh-bone
of a great bear, preserved
for millennia in a dry cave?
Broken at both ends, it is a flute,
three holes punched evenly
along its brown and hollow length.

Someone helped this bear
to find an honorable death,
then fashioned its femur
to sing of rock and ice,
and of the hot blood
blessing his cold hands
as he lifted its warm flesh
toward the stars of an ancient sky.

If we would call bear home,
we must leave this relic
in the cave, then sit
for years in its mouth
until the bear's rank breath
courses through our bones.

[a drum beat, a heart beat]

On the wall
of a cave, artists
painted animals
millions of years ago

[a drum beat, a heart beat]

A severe thunderstorm
threatened my return
to the family; I heard
a familiar voice, and
decided to explore the cave,
finding the voice which called.

I couldn't see my hands,
my feet, my body, and
I panicked.

[a drum beat, a heart beat]

Black Bear greeted me,
calmed me, protected me
from dangers when traveling
from dangers faced daily
Black Bear said, You have
chosen this path, and should
not be afraid when you confront
yourself, your internal light
will guide you. Black Bear
blended into the darkness

I wanted to bathe in the rain,
to feel the sun, to touch the dew
on the grass, the leaves

I wanted to run

Black Bear's spiritual presence
nudged me forward, and with each
step I became confident

the internal light cast shadows
on the walls

adulthood, adolescence, childhood
a baby held in my parents' arms

The voice I recognized

I became/I am

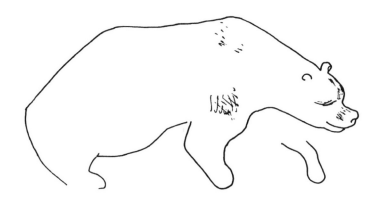

Going Back

Shiraoi
Ainu village
in the midst of
Americanized Japan
the scenery around
like Oregon.
Heavy mist.
Mountains.
Lush dark green.
The sense of an
unsayable truth
behind,
hiding in the evergreen forest.

Some Ainu people
heavily intermarried with Japanese
heavy dark bodies and square heavy faces

dance
in a round
one male intermittently slashes
with a sword
imitating the motions
of sea animals or
bears in
black cloth with white
square pattern

reminiscent of the Haida and
Tlingit

animal sound songs
Sioux tremolos
sweet Polynesian trills
sweeping their arms down
bears
hauling
fishing nets

moving backwards
stepping
bears,
beautiful bears
gods of the Ainu in human form
come down to earth,

soon to be "slain,"

going back.

"Ainu" The Ainu are to the Japanese what the American Indians are to the United States, the natives who got pushed back and eliminated as another people moved in. They were the original inhabitants of the Japanese archipelago. Believed by some to be an isolated group of Caucasians, because many of the men have large beards, Ainu religion centers around the bear. They believe it to be their duty to kill bears because the bear is a god trying to return to heaven. The only way is through death. The "killing," however, is a ritual one in which the bear is treated with every decency. Most Ainu today live on the northern island of Hakkaido.

Robert M. Chute

From his long poem

Black Mink Loses His Balance

V. Balancing

Far North, far South, white river snakes,
hills wrap forest over breast, thighs, knees.
Black ant-people creep across the lake,
reach the wide white lake's further side,
are shadows in shadow under trees.

The Raven somersaults, then glides
over drifting smoke in springs of air.
Raven's feather fingers are spread wide,
his scavenging eye becomes the sky.
The patient forest is the bear.

Laura Snyder

Apple Tree

my outstretched shirt
is pregnant with apples
I carry them full term
to deliver you from black bear.

Sheila Nickerson

The Mountain That Holds Bears: October

The trails of the bears
fill up with ice, with rain.
Underground, rivers flow,
their power rising
like nightfall from the sea.
The mountain settles into snow,
opening its pockets for things of fur.
Turning home, I leave no trail.
If we meet – guests of this terrain –
and if we touch, it will be to know
the immensity of mountains:
the miracle of where our feet come down.

Song of the Black Bear

My moccasins are black obsidian,
My leggings are black obsidian,
My shirt is black obsidian.
I am girded with a black arrowsnake.
Black snakes go up from my head.
With zigzag lightning darting from the ends of my feet
    I step,
With zigzag lightning streaming out from my knees
    I step,
With zigzag lightning streaming from the tip of my tongue
    I speak.
Now a disk of pollen rests on the crown of my head.
Gray arrowsnakes and rattlesnakes eat it.
Black obsidian and zigzag lightning streams out
    from me in four ways,
Where they strike the earth, bad things, bad talk
    does not like it.
It causes the missiles to spread out.
Long life, something frightful I am.
Now I am.

There is danger where I move my feet.
I am whirlwind.
There is danger when I move my feet.
I am a gray bear.
When I walk, where I step, lightning flies from me,
Where I walk, one to be feared (I am).
Where I walk, Long Life.
One to be feared I am.
There is danger where I walk.

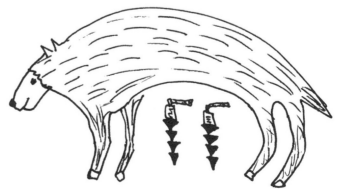

Hazards of Photography

Smack on his back in the snow,
as if he might stretch his thick legs
to make an angel, the bear is dead,
stripped of stomach and fur.
The hunter, Yuji Shiramata,
takes a picture with his new Nikon.
It is his first bear and his last.
In two days another bear will tear
the focus out of Yuji's eyes
and leave him stumbling to his death
in Akita Prefecture. The bear
will sing of it deep in his throat
and stand on his hind legs
growling like an old man
having his picture taken.

Under the Skin

The skin of the bear cub that Kozlov gave me
like the shirt off his back
from his bleak bedroom wall in Leningrad

bred moths on my Ohio office wall
until I returned it to the forest
beyond the field behind my house

toting a ladder through corn stubble
to the highest, fattest tree
which I ascended armed with a staple gun

to help the cub hug the rough bark once more —
its arms spread wide like black mittens,
head flung back as if to cry for mother

before my final act of crucifixion. Kozlov joked
that the cub had not been killed in Siberia
but in a park along the Nevsky Prospect

where artists now are free to peddle kitsch:
Meester! Oh, Meester! I have what you like!
Special for you! Meester! Then from Aipin

who hunted and fished with his father
in Khanty-Mansiisk I learned how they
Dance the Bear with solemn myth-songs,

an invitation from deep forest to grand
feast. One of the elders cloaked in bear-
skin is announced from the outskirts of the

village by the sound of a bell (five for a He-
Bear, four for a She, the Females bedecked
in jewelry) while the others chant and sing

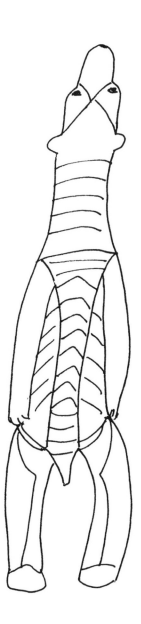

continued on next page

Kyingem-Yeingem! Chovie-Chovie!
Then for five days ancient rituals claim all:
sport, food, jest, song, incantation, rest,

and *Kyingem-Yeingem! Chovie-Chovie!*
The words are old and untranslatable.
Their purpose is to Dance the old Bear home.

Premonition

A hard shiver
on an August afternoon
on the screened porch, book
full of forest and shipwreck on my knees.

Two men have set off in a canoe, in white water,
to test their skill.
Elsewhere, a young couple
pack their baby into bear country.

Have we had enough hero stories?
Is there a *märchen,* somewhere in Grimm,
about giving babies to bears, or
am I thinking of an American story
of transformation, children sent to be
bears, stronger and safer than children?

At nightfall, the men explain —
the canoe flipped, rolled in the rapids.
One tells how he came up under it, fought free,
fished gear out onto the river bank,
netted the wallets that a plastic bag buoyed up.
They spread the money to dry on the dinner table.

In the morning, we hear how the grizzly
dropped on all fours and disappeared
up the path.

I thought I would be more patient
at this age.

Totem

In my dream
the Great Bear stands,
paws and head raised up in prayer –
then falls
soundlessly
while those who gather to witness
circle him in silence,
slowed by awe.

Who am I here –
watcher of watchers,
heart as blank as paper.
Isis would weep,
Inanna howl to heaven,
Ereshkigal gnash her teeth to tear.

I focus my film.
Have I ordered his death –
my Great Bear
with his fur like fire
over my frozen fingers,
over my icy heart?

To the Bear

"After your paw was shot off,
Didn't Nature become one-handed,
Didn't Nature become half-handed?"

"Through the rifle muzzle
Aimed at you,
Looking back out of the taiga forest
Attentively,
Do you think us improved?"

A TAIGA NENETS DRAWING

Translated and Edited from Vaella's poem "The Bear Feast" by Alexander
Vaschenko of Moscow State University and Claude Clayton Smith of Ohio
Northern University for inclusion in *The Way of Kinship*, an anthology of Native
Siberian literature.

Those who have packed far up into grizzly country know that the presence of even one grizzly on the land elevates the mountains, deepens the canyons, chills the winds, brightens the stars, darkens the forest and quickens the pulse of all who enter it. They know that when a bear dies, something sacred in every living thing interconnected with that realm . . . also dies.

John Murray

To Kill The Distance Between

THE YOUNG MEN did not want the old man to hunt with them, but they let him come along. All along the journey they made fun of him, saying how slow and useless he was. Suddenly, a grizzly bear charged them from behind a dark bush and all the young men turned and ran, leaving the old man alone to face the hungry bear. When it was very close the old man yelled and waved his arms. That grizzly didn't know what to think, so he just stopped right there and sat down. The old man wasted no time. He smacked the bear across his tender nose and the great bear turned and ran away.

—from a Tanacross myth

Flames

Smokey the Bear heads
into the autumn woods
with a red can of gasoline
and a box of wooden matches.

His ranger's hat is cocked
at a disturbing angle.

His brown fur gleams
under the high sun
as his paws, the size
of catchers' mitts,
crackle into the distance.

He is sick of dispensing
warnings to the careless,
the half-wit camper,
the dumbbell hiker.

He is going to show them
how a professional does it.

David Smith-Ferri ———————————————

Worker for Hire
for Diego

moving,
ursine, through the underbrush
  brother to a bear,
      the machete, a tooth,

  insatiable,
tearing at scotch broom,
  at oak and manzanita
  chipping bone
    spilling blood.

Janell Moon ———————————————

Bear

Little boy in the bear suit,
pawing at butterflies, scratching
your back on the birch.
Your daddy is 1500 pounds
or is he the man eating
tuna salad at the kitchen table.
Oh, you on your hind legs, you are
scaring the baby.

David Allan Evans ———————————————

Feeding the Bears

when
some day at
feeding time the
Grizzly
springs up over his wall

catch the
look
on the face of
the man who feeds
the animals

The Bear

Who would burn a bear   with cigarettes
and yet they did   over and over
at the city park   under the cottonwoods
brown bear with   much of its fur missing
next to the bandstand   it didn't know to go
to the center of its cage   it kept pacing
the way they do   rubbing itself
against the bars   shuffle turn
shuffle back   the small flames I imagined
clinging to its fur   were my own first matches
over the toilet bowl   wooden soldiers
with their red caps first   then black I loved
the flash and fizzle   flushing them down
afterwards but no one   heard the bear
or came to see   maybe it didn't scream
old anyway   missing its teeth
so they went right on   when we heard the explosion
we were still eating Well   my father said
they've shot the bear   one hand on his water glass
the big fingers opening   and closing

The Ring
A Nocturne
> *north of Los Angeles, 1850*

To kill the distance between
beasts is what Pedro desires.
The grizzly, chained, roars fierce with wild.
Its fangs disdain the men, sunk black to color,
behind the bars, who whoop and scream
in languages myriad. The sun
refrains to warm this place, greased
by milling men. The air hangs under yells
for blood as the bull heads toward the ring.
Pedro knows a grand jealousy is what
the gringos feel toward them. And Mexico
grows realer men. The torches strain the glow.
The gate releases. The bull fears death
but charges toward its belly.
The grizzly slaps at its attack,
and profit rings the air/
                         a lunge/
                    a dodge/
            a bite sinks deep/
                  a horn finds tender flesh/
and fur and meat become as one,
like Chinaman and Jew. Christian
and the Indian both slaver at the spectacle,
wipe blood that dowses them/
                      a heave/
                a moan/
              co-mingling of the strains
              repairs the lapse to care/
                          a vessel sliced/
                  a tendon snapped/
                      bone meets bone
                      as bone gives way/
                pain abounds/
        within the men/
     and/
out/

back at the beginning of civilizing
such sights were seeds of myth.
Now, time and gold have blanched
them through – they reek a commonness.
No one can differentiate the race
of men behind the bars. The grizzly does not care
as the bull breathes deep its own release.
The bear limps slowly into dark. Cheers
abound, with scattered boos, some things
find newer hands. And Pedro heads home,
to his bunk this night, as the galaxies
slide further and further away.

The Bear

Thrown from the boxcar of the train, the bear
rolls over and over. He sits up
rubbing his nose. This must be
some mistake,
                there is no audience here.
He shambles off through the woods.
The forest is veined with trails,
he does not know which to follow.
The wind is rising, maple leaves turn up
their silver undersides in agony, there is a
smell in the air, and the lightning strikes.
He climbs a tree to escape. The rain
pours down, the bear is blue as a gall.

       . . .

There is not much to eat
in the forest, only berries,
and some small delicious animals
that live in a mound and bite your nose.

       . . .

The bear moves sideways through a broom-straw field
He sees the hunters from the corner of his eye
and is sure they have come to take him back.
To welcome them, (though there is no calliope)
he does his somersaults, and juggles
a fallen log, and something
tears through his shoulder,
he shambles away in the forest and cries.
Do they not know who he is?

       . . .

After a while, he learns to fish, to find
the deep pool and wait for the silver trout.
He learns to keep his paw up for spiderwebs.
There is only one large animal, with trees
on its head, that he cannot scare.

. . .

At last he is content to be
alone in the forest,
though sometimes he finds a clearing
and solemnly does his tricks,
though no one sees.

N. RUDIN

The Bears of Paris

The wind, a moving cipher
to the civilized, tells tales to bears
of silver salmon winking juicy eyes
at the *poissonnerie*, of honey and jam
liberated from jars, of wine and sweet pastries.
It carries these forbidden smells
along the Rue Linné

to where danger hulks like brown, furry mountains
at the Ménagerie of the Jardin des Plantes.
The bears of Paris measure their stone holes
with heavy, daggered steps:

Children stand tiptoe at the spiked-iron fence
to stare and point at tongues
licking guillotine fangs, at ursine eyes
glazing over with thoughts of dinner.

When the children run home, the red candy sun
bowing before them, the bears are left
to gnaw rocky bones in their pit Bastille.
The moon shines a Conciergerie spotlight
on those too wild for sweets and freedom;
the wind growls in the chestnut trees,
bringing night messages for bears to dream
of forests, venison, caves and blood.

Thinking Too Much: The Dancing Bear

It was Greek tragedy, the dancing bear
shot dead for dragging off a sleeping bag:
the bag turned into a giant jumping bean
which turned into a scream sprouting a kid.

The kid's RED HOTS. Bear thought them his.
Earlier Bear had waltzed the center ring,
dancing in circles for the whip's Kisses,
his shoulders gliding like a trapeze swing.

      Then later he escapes
      and tries to camp
      out with the RED
      HOTS Kid, who won't

      share the yummies.
      The bear gets smart,
      this leads to that,
      and he gets whacked:

Ranger shows up, and there's our camping bear
with a hand on his hip like a beer mug,
waltzes toward the Ranger. Friendly creature,
this bruin, laid out like a bear rug.

The bars of his cage had been his trapeze
net. But left open, no way he'd get caught
if he fell through, someone gets hurt. Pure Greek,
how to avoid the hole, he went through it.

red velvet swing

i remember
seeing the
trained bear
sitting on
a swing
in north carolina,
and even as i
smiled,
something cracked
in my heart.
why must we
bring all the great creatures
down to our level,
only because we are
not capable of rising to theirs?
annie lamott says
one of the secrets
of life is having
a giant panda
in your backyard
just to make you smile.
perfect in theory,
except some damn fool
would shoot it.
bears and bunnies energize;
pandas, save us and make wise.

On the Day of the Fair

Today was for watching the bear.
A peasant boy,
With tufts of white-blond hair
Sticking out from his embroidered cap,
Held a honied pirok in his hand
And chewed with studied deliberation,
As he stared at the toddling beast
And wiped his nose on his sleeve.
It reared its paws into the air
And moaned a song to its trainer's lash,
Then raised its eyes to the sky
And brayed in pain at the sun.

Then, it looked down,
Brown eyes met the boy's blue,
And beast seemed to plead to child.
The market square's mute wooded walls
Mixed their scent of pine
With the smoke of roasting meat,
And that lost day, and that lost life
Faded into the trees and plains,
As the boy stood and stared, amazed,
And the forest brute beat his heavy chains.

July's Arctic Bears

"I want to see the bears." I said
that day, July 1957
when my father took my hand
half-pulling, half leading me from the
dry hot summer up winding marble stairs
turning and rising higher to a cavernous hall,
the world where we walked and walked
below the molded ceiling sky
past South America   past Savannah   to the Arctic
the end of the world.

There were the polar bears   huge white bodies in frozen snow encased in glass
my body hot, my hand sweaty in my father's, my heart beating fast,
the baby polar bear with fish in its mouth,
father back, waiting.
The baby and I were eye to eye.
Red-pink lines shone at the edge of the sunset in the middle of day where
we were all bathed in the pale blue light at the end of the wing,
my father and the baby polar bear and the father polar bear and I.

I thought if we stood long enough we would be the bears

and here we are, in fact,
remembering our history on a July day neither I, nor he,
would ever have imagined forty years ago.
My father and I walk slowly
as we retrace steps taken before
in the world, entombed in the familiar cavern where we had walked
before my father turned eighty.
The Arctic bears are frozen, standing still in red-pink lines at the edge of sunset
the fish in the baby bear's mouth,
the father waiting,
my eyes looking down at the baby bear
encased in pale blue light.

Bear Day

Wednesdays Alice visits the bear.
She packs herself a nice tuna sandwich,
pops on her broad-brimmed straw hat,
watches the browning ivy pass
outside the window of the freeway express.

At the zoo gate
she shows her senior citizen discount pass
like the visa to a foreign land.

Today the bear is hiding
dark in the concrete den.
Alice waits on her concrete bench
under the yellow acacia
at the gray bank of the unforested moat.

The plastic wrapping of her sandwich
glistens like writhing trout.
Her food tastes like sweet grass and summer berries,
smells like wild honey comb,
spicy as red ants,
gamey as a felled deer.

Alice nestles herself
into the cave of green shade.
Leaves are thick as hair of a fat beast.
She closes her eyes:
She is furless and without sight like a cub
new-dropped out of her mother's black sleep.

Alice pulls herself thirty feet below winter,
nuzzles the pelt of day.

The Day Weeders

A big paw swats a small rump.
Parent and child roll over
And around and into each other,
Looking happy and harmless.
In my slow ignorance
I see them as merely simple,
Easy-going, sunlit and pretty.
It is late in the day
Before I comprehend
What is really going on:

The zoo bears are living on dreams.
They are weeding through the days.
They are putting on a show,
A lazy-daisy performance,
Thinking that if they make us
Laugh, we will forgive them
For wishing they were home;
Thinking that if they amuse us,
Let us think that wild-yearning
Has been replaced by love for us,
That we will come off guard just long
Enough to spring them free.

The Window at the Polar Bear Exhibit

has a small hole in the putty seal.
I've been standing for thirty minutes
watching a white bear sleeping.
His left foot lies by a pile of shit
and the rest of him lies fast asleep.
Babies in strollers speed past,
"He's asleep. Let's go." But I wait.

My wife, who painted the bears
last week, told me about it.
She told how the bear had played,
pushed a ball into the water
then turned and walked back
to her, watched her sketch his arms
and then he blew his breath
into the window hole.

Bears are made of the same dust as we, and breathe the same winds and drink of the same waters. A bear's days are warmed by the same sun, his dwellings are overdomed by the same blue sky, and his life turns and ebbs with heart-pulsings like ours and was poured from the same fountain.
John Muir

Waiting For The Bear

THE INDIAN GIRL ran as fast as she could from the bear, but it was faster and would soon catch her. She prayed and prayed as she ran. Then, all of a sudden, the rocky ground around her started moving. It started lifting her towards the sky, higher and higher. As the rock rose, the bear tried to climb up to the girl, but his claws only scratched the rock. Finally, the bear turned and left, leaving behind long scratches in the rock which is now called Devil's Tower.

– from a Cheyenne & Crow myth

You Are in Bear Country

Advice from a pamphlet published by the
Canadian Minister of the Environment

They've
been here
for thousands of years.
You're
the visitor.
Avoid
encounters. Think ahead.
Keep clear
of berry patches
garbage dumps, carcasses.
On woods walks bring
noisemakers, bells.
Clap hands along the trail
or sing
but in dense bush
or by running water
bear may not hear your clatter.
Whatever else
don't whistle. Whistling
is thought by some to imitate
the sounds bears make when they mate.

You need to know
there are two kinds:
ursus arctus horribilis
or grizzly
and *ursus americanus*
the smaller black
said to be
somewhat less likely to attack.
Alas, a small *horribilis*
is difficult to distinguish
from a large *americanus*.

Although
there is no
guaranteed life-saving way

continued on next page

to deal with an aggressive bear
some ploys
have proved more
successful than others.
Running's a poor choice.
Bear can outrun a racehorse.

Once you're face to face
speak softly. Take
off your pack
and set it down
to distract the grizzly.
Meanwhile back
slowly toward a large
sparsely branched tree
but remember
black bears are agile climbers
in which case
a tree may not offer escape.

As a last resort you can
play dead. Drop
to the ground face down.
In this case
wearing your pack
may shield your body from attack.
Courage. Lie still. Sometimes
your bear may veer away.
If not
bears have been known
to inflict only minor injuries
upon the prone.

*Is death
by bear to be preferred
to death by bomb?* Under
these extenuating circumstances
your mind may make absurd
leaps. *The answer's yes.*
Come on in. Cherish
your wilderness.

Waiting for the Bear

For Bill

Alone this time, I raise the patched tent, weigh
the corners down with granite half-moons and fists.

In San Francisco you are trying to sit up,
loose skin above the red incision gathered
into a grey pouch beneath your chin.
Last week they sawed through ribs, the brittle
insistent arcs of bone and, lifting your heart
in gloved hands, attached the new veins.
I was there with your wife before you woke up.
I have not touched your chest since our
grown daughters were in nursery school.

Eighteen summers in the high Sierra.
Half wild with fear, I acted the father's part,
loading sleeping bags and camp stoves
into my car, telling our girls that the world
was safe, that they could do anything.
Lakes blue-green above the tree line,
thunderheads blooming behind Ebbott's Pass,
the split-second texture of lightning.
Range cattle lowered their horns
and chased us down the Mosquito Creek trail.
Those summers I nursed an angry joy
at being able to do it all without you.
Nights were terrifying. I waited for the bear.

Eighteen years a Sunday father, you were good
at making brunch and driftwood fires. Our daughters
sprawled in your enormous pillows, reading.
You were good at the helm of a boat gauging
the lift and slide of water, danger still something
you courted too, the girls along for the ride.

continued on next page

The bear patrolled his territory each August.
Crescent moon balanced above the incense cedar,
full moon whitening dogwood leaves,
no moon, wind crooning across solid rock, he came
not as wild spirit but as a reckoning.
How had I dared try to raise these girls alone?
Once the bear ripped two cars open
as we watched. Most years he simply walked by.

I chose places where I couldn't phone
to hear you say *Everything will be all right.*
We went higher and higher, packed up to Matthes Lake
miles beyond Tuolumne Meadows, slept on stone,
trip lines strung with drinking cups linking our packs together.
Stars wheeled above us and when he came
his footsteps shook the granite. It felt
as if we had spread our bodies on a drum.

Now, no children to protect, the woods hold nothing
to keep me awake. I think of you
in that hospital, how the years deprive us
of our fondest grudges, our most elaborate fears.
Tonight, no tin cups banging, no reprieves,
the massive feet shuffling away. You and I are both waiting.
Oh, my dear friend, it is not the bear who comes.

My Father's Heart, the Doctor Says,
No Longer Beats, But Quivers

On hind legs through pond water, the huge cinnamon grizzly labors to reach us on the front porch. The way my father wades through fluid in his lungs to reach each breath. *Go inside,* he whispers. *Go slowly.* The air quivers on the tide of grizzly breath. I put on my shoes, fumble with the laces, go inside. Peer through the door's blurred glass as the bear ascends our steps, see my father rise to meet him. The grizzly grins, pulls my father's body into his. I can no longer see my father's face. His arms go out around the grizzly's torso, as though they had been groping for the shape of this moment. He bows his head into the fur's deep nap.

Night Visitor

There where I had camped at dusk,
Death walked into the clearing
doubled over on all fours
in the guise of a great bear.

I had not eaten all day,
but had not fasted
to bring about that vision.
Nevertheless, it would now unfold
in four parts, as it must.

I.   Like a child, I was delighted
     to see the bear,
     as if our stuffed animal
     had finally come alive
     the way we always knew it could
     if it wanted to.

II. But as I stood motionless
     in the doorway of my tent,
     fear sweeping suddenly through me
     took me nearly to the ground.

III. That towards which
     we all reluctantly move
     had that night moved towards me.
     The knife in my hand was very small,
     but I was ready then, and calm.

IV. The bear padded slowly
     past my tent and me
     as if we were not there.
     The thin nylon wall
     hung between our worlds like a veil.

Now years later as I tell this,
I realize the bear is always there
at the edge of the clearing;
the knife is always too small.
The joy is in pitching my tent
over and over again
to wait for the morning
whether it comes or not.

Co-Existing

"To him everything is food except granite."
— John Muir of the grizzly

Thin membrane of tent holds us
in mountain meadow, hours between
   dark and light
to sleep. Under our shoulder-blades press
tubers, roots, bears' food.
Our hands move on the mounds where seeds,
developing below ground, vulnerable
   as little breasts,
shudder and tremble as they swell from within.
Ear against earth, we wake to hear
movements through meadow grass
that makes us know our own
fleshy smell is meat.

Our teeth as bears' teeth, took
those bitter berries bitten in the sun,
whose shell still spreads a tartness on the tongue.
We cooked the rabbit at the campfire, ate,
then, leaped and swam, curving as fish, upstream.
   Water slid, sparkling, from the
bear's fur, his paw scooped the silver fish,
arcing through sun. The bear
ambles on rodent path
and rabbit run in meadow grass.
Flesh of the rabbit quivers. Membrane of
 skin torn.

Cataracts

Their meetings in clearings
Were never matters of words
But of light and dark enclosing them.
Toward the end of winter
Fog hovers above the cabin
When evening comes.
He goes out to wander,
To shake a blizzard he sees
Where no snow has fallen in weeks.

In the clearing the dark form appears,
Passes quickly, is lost in night brush.
He has seen the bear again.
It has been weeks since the last time.

He follows the image through branches
That scratch skin and memory
Of all winters, of a bear
Too blurred to shoot,
Too fast, too much alive.

He has sought the bear for six Springs
Increasingly vague, with decreased certainty.
He has held out despite frailty,
Hoping for meetings
Within the arm of chance.
Once, in a hollow, they came face to face
And he let his rifle drop.
Even what he wanted to say abandoned him.
Now he wants another chance.
This time, words will not fail him.

Darkness coats the damp trail, evergreens,
Even the backs of his hands.
Finally he reaches the hollow,

continued on next page

Makes an effort to memorize it.
The next time, he will be less sure of it,
Of most things.

He is stood up.
This night, there will be no meeting,
Only two beings wandering the night,
Solitude the one thing they share.
He wishes for light, for bearing.
For a long time he stands there,
Then turns to go.

The Fitchburg Bear

Given the path of lapped-out garbage cans
and bird feeders rich with months-old,
unvisited suet, he came out of Lunenburg Forest,
down Lunenburg Street. Before that, no one
can imagine, this being a most civilized state,
we know, having spent the day tracking
Joseph Palmer, old iconoclast, jailed
for a year for growing a beard and expelled
from Fruitlands for drinking milk.
We can imagine how Alcott would feel
about doughnuts fried in some animal's deep grease.

But this bear was no ursine Emerson,
lumbering in to lecture in Fitchburg.
And unlike the Vermont moose who fell in love
with a cow and mooned at the fence for days,
the bear did not fall for a sheepdog or Rottweiler.
This was the James Beard of bears, a bear
as gormandish as Siri, the India elephant who invented
this recipe for hay: step on an orange or apple
gently, rub fruit into straw, and serve.
He came to dine.

As happy as the gorillas who sing during dinner,
the bear wandered into the Bernardian Bowl,
maybe for the just desserts of track meets,
followed by police, ordered to shoot if the bear
got to Main Street, with all of its restaurants.
The citizens, intent that he'd live free not die,
ducked in and out of the gun sights, shouting
Save our bear, leaving the police in a quandary
of how to keep the bear and not kill anyone.
The solution was so obvious I'm embarrassed,
but what do police care of triteness and narrative?

They sent out for two dozen doughnuts
that held the bear at bay one cake at a time.
He'd gulp one down, then sit back on his haunches,

continued on next page

just like a bear I saw once standing at the grill
of a family cowering in their car
while the Smoky Mountain native spiked
each of their hotdogs on a claw. He kissed one
to his mouth like a cocktail treat, rested,
kissed and rested ten times.
While the Fitchburg bear ate,
animal wardens were arriving with stun guns.

After an hour they hauled him
as he hibernated out of season
to Quabbin Reservoir—dreaming the bear dream
equal of an assignment to review Main Street cafes.
When he woke to twigs and berries
he had to wonder which was the dream.
Unlike Segismundo, he had the evidence,
the suet and doughnuts still slick
on his tongue, in his nose, the smell
of humans, stuffing him.

Folsom Street Rain

I see you in the rain,
tall bear,
the wet dripping down your hair
like Clark Gable.
You come to me in a poem.
We stood on Folsom Street
wrapped in a long hug,
tall bear,
your head in the trees
your long arms reaching down.
We swayed in the wind,
back and forth in the wind,
wrapped in tree branches.
You reached up
and plucked stars
as if they were apples.

Bears of Cheyenne Canyon

This October a host of silent bears
has come to Cheyenne Canyon
as never before.
Tonight's canyon bear almost looks like
Miles Davis from his *In a Silent Way* days;
black face, black eyes, brown skin tints
and a black mass surrounding his huge,
shiny head, making it appear
as if the bear had some *Round*
Midnight riffs in his walking away sound,
as if Miles with his late night horn
was playing rhythms endlessly
into this mammalian's dark
dancing path of experience
and crossing sounds of the night
into sentences
before ears or bears
know best where to bend.

Even this sleepy, city kid
can watch those quiet
lumbering swatches of huge darkness
kindly cross his asphalt street.
In their hungry-eyed stares of wonder,
he thinks these creatures could eat him so easily,
though they want only to rifle and gobble garbage
and amaze us with their ghostly humility
of what the hibernating winter in their blood
needs to become—some dreaming scene
of humans lumbering away, walking
on their tongues and tasting
the truth of earth.

Out Picking Berries

of whatever kind I could find
was a northwoods thing, just fun to do
in my youth before my fear of mosquitoes
attacking through the talltrees shadows
grew to what it is today

back then I'd heard tell there were bears around
from what the country folk liked to rumor
and on occasion they'd caught cougars & wolves
skulking from tree-stands to fields
but this talk didn't worry me.

one time exploring, you can't imagine my thrill
when tall-grass-deep in a hollow
between the shaded coolnesses
coming across a gigantic cache of black
like I'd never seen before
ten-feet-tall bushes
swaying their weight way bent over
in the midst of this trail-less solitude

what a great blackberry patch!
I whooped to rebounding woods echoes
how I could have it mostly to myself
(if I'd pick fast enough to beat the birds)
thinking of their exquisite taste
as I sampled some
and of the many oozing pies to come
thinking of the many mornings having them
tumble over my breakfast flakes
dark thimbles mingling in mounds of brown

except that suddenly I sensed
I was not alone
glimpsed a roundbrown furry shape lingering near

continued on next page

asking questions with its eyes —
my initial half-surprise impulse was to
dash away for safety's sake

but remembering what grandpa had said
that usually bears are a bit scared too
I stayed my ground
in the back of my mind knowing
I'd probably never find my way back here again
to this treasure trove of a lifetime

so as it turned out
there was not a double crashing retreat
and I got both my buckets full
of my favorite wild-growing fruit

and best, as time went on I knew I had gotten
a first-class story to tell
so many times over, whenever the chance
reserved in my mind for grandchildren too —
but above all else standing out
remembering about the curious something
I'd seen in its big bear eyes
for that suspended instant it lingered

ROBYN BERGSMA

Grrrrr

The Bear on the New Red Road

Here in these hills, nothing
but trees and a few neighbors
scattered like dry leaves. A long swinging
drive from my city comforts. Lonely.
Lonely. I prayed that some day they'd plant
pavement here. A string of stores
would sprout like neat rows of pine. And then
as if in answer, trucks shambled up our dusty
street, and cleared the trees aside. I climbed

the new red road, my hope,
cheering the progress as clean
blond boards translated the
terrain to a language I spoke. Banks
of defeated leaves, twigs, trunks, tangled
mess of broken beehives, circled
the site. A clearing against confusion.
At last.

Until he appeared
crawling along the not-yet lawn
of Lot Number Eight. All I was was scared.
My heart raced while he held my stare. I was home
too quick to notice his snout was cinnamon brown,
his fat black coat hung on round shoulders.
I was safe when I shut my door. My lair of
glass and locks. Knobs he couldn't turn.

While I slept, he returned. His shoulders
sinking closer to the ground as he inspected. Searched
the lot for wasps nests he'd swung open
last season, the apple tree
whose branches he'd toppled gathering
sweets, the ditch he rolled in to chase flies
from his back. Nothing familiar. The stripped
wood, straight, smooth and useless
smelled of another lonely creature.

continued on next page

He reached high on the face of a bordering tree
scraped his nails down the bark
till it bled sweet and sticky.
Rubbed his back against it. Rubbed
his shaggy smell into the tree
mixing his fur with its sap. Singing
I am here. I am here.

Apples and Bears

That summer, after our Mexican divorce,
I cut Tamarack for the garden fence
intended to keep the deer out.

Most times, I would forget to eat
or sleep, talk to myself, feed our dogs
from the table, swim naked at midnight
in a lake full of stars.

Once, still restless after my swim,
I wandered barefoot down the sun warmed
talc road to the abandoned orchard alive
with Red Delicious, Granny Smiths and Jonagolds,
where I found a bear cub caught in an apple tree
crying in the moonlight.

His paws so full of red sweetness
could not give up their happiness
to maneuver back down the old tree.
So there he sat bawling into the night,
his joy creating his sorrow.

A salient reminder of my own choices:
deer and Tamarack, dusty roads in moonlight,
star filled lakes, apples and bears, even
though it means a life without you.

Autumn, Bears and Apple Trees

In the time when leaves are divided yellow
from green, bears descend to grub
apples from our scattered trees. They climb
with grace, standing man-like on two shaggy
haunches, lift horned paws to grasp
the scent of wind in frost blushed apples.
Indiscriminate browsers, they pull leaves
and branches toward their hunger. Higher they stretch,
they snag the apples we could not reach.

Five trees mark out the compass points
of the bears' nightly route. Gathering beads
of night dew, course black manes brush
paths through summer-baked timothy and fescue,
push past thorns and red-rounded hips of wild roses:
the bears pass with one mind. In black of night
the dog awakes, bear scent stuffs her nostrils
flares that special bark, which says *Bear.*
Bear, Bear, . . .Bear, Bear! Bear turns
his woolly head at his name being called,
then turns back to feed his craving.

Each year we try to beat the bears
from their ripe apples. But in their lust
they find each hidden fruit we miss.
Each year they climb, each year they test
the creaking branches, and each year
break a few more, pruning
according to some bear wisdom.
Still the scraggly trees survive,
though the branches seem broken past life,
and in spring bloom through splinted wings.

Bush League

Afloat in low space
among canes both thicketed and barbed,
a spotless baseball cap
hovers, its divisions
of orange and black
domed above the bill,
above the black berries.

As I watch, it rises,
like a Blackstone trick,
until brown fur and cocked ears
present the head of a bear
on whose mountain it perches
ridiculous
  delicious.

How it got there;
why it stays there,
unknown, at least to me,
and he declines to say.

After a moment of point-counterpoint
I say, *I guess you know*
they won today.
A soft *wuh,*
and he subsides
and goes his way.

Spared

we picked a spot in the woods
set up camp
cooked dinner
something greasy
the yellow jackets swarmed
around the frying pan
so badly we put it on the other
side of some rocks outside camp

after the fire had died down
the story had been told
one after another
we slipped away to our beddings

the moon had looked away
felt a tremor in the ground
something heavy
heard it move through camp
thought of Sasquatch
too frightened to move

stopped next to me
long moments of sniffing
on the other side of my tent
I stared fear into the blackness
then felt the canvas bow inward
tremendous weight moved me
more sniffs
another nudge
and my silent prayer to god of all
the things I'd meant to do
but never did

the hulk must have heard
the prayer
stopped
sniffed and left
one heavy foot after another.

In the morning
I found the huge bear tracks
put my hand inside an imprint
followed them
to the black iron frying pan nearly
licked clean of last night
except one buzzing yellow jacket
trapped in solid grease
its prayer heard
spared as I had been.

On a Night Without Moon

You probably walked pigeon-toed
across the road on a night without moon

following some delicious scent,
when it happened.,
When the beast with blazing eyes lunged.

Perhaps the driver saw and tried to stop.
Perhaps your black shape blended with the road.

A bump, and the truck went on,
driver bouncing to a hard-rock beat.

You crawled from there to here,
wondered why you could not walk.

How long did you lie in this ditch
before hearing stopped,

before the smell of berries a yard away stopped,
before the feel of metal-monster-rumble stopped
on the hard, straight path, before you rose up
out of your body to follow your constellation?

Now I address your matted black fur,
white bone, canines clenched in death grin.

Now I dare pick up your claws,
hold them to the light,
reflect that Indians wear them
as symbols of bravery.

I say to you, bear, I am not brave.
I am a thief stealing thunder.

I wanted to see you walk a forest path,
fish a pool like an old man.

But all I see is vacant carcass,
your hunter heart has vanished
somewhere beyond the moon.

Bear in Taos Cycle

Terry Kiraly describes the events of last Friday evening:

I'm in front of my store – Taos Cycle – & my foster son, Tate
Gonzales, is in the back when, real casual, around 7 P.M., this
bear walks in.

Tate calls to me that a brown bear is in the building.
I laugh & say sure. But it really is a bear – a good-sized cub.

I open the door, but the bear doesn't want to leave.
Then I think it might walk out on the highway
or head for town
& cause real trouble.
So I ask my wife Patty to call New Mexico State Police.

They refer us to Taos Police, the Fish & Game Department,
Animal Control Officer Jerry Padilla, & U.S. Forest Service.

Police officer Damasco Martinez arrives first & tries to
tranquilize the cub, shooting two darts into it. A third dart
fails to penetrate. Then the goddamn gun runs out of gas.
Martinez suggest getting a rope
putting it around the bear's neck
& pulling it out of the shop
by means of human strength.

But by this time the Fish & Game men have arrived
& advise against this. A bear climbs trees & fights
with its claws & teeth, says one. If you put a rope
around his neck, he'll just run up the rope & attack you.
What we need is a snare & a pole – to keep the animal back.

So we send for a snare & a pole.

continued on next page

When Damasco Martinez
puts the snare around the bear's neck, it begins to fight
jumping on snowmobiles & motorcycles & knocking some
over. Martinez tightens the snare but the cub continues
to fight, making choking noises.

After a while, the cub loses consciousness.

Then Jerry Padilla takes over. He puts him
in the Animal Control truck & takes off the snare & pole.
By now there's a crowd of spectators. We all stand around
the truck waiting for the animal to regain consciousness.

But he doesn't.

Someone thinks of shining a flashlight on his pupils
but they don't dilate. Finally, Martinez takes off his heavy
leather gloves & feels the bear's heart with his naked hand.
He can't find a pulse. So Martinez
pronounces the bear dead
puts his glove back on
gets in gear
& drives away.

My store lost about 200 dollars in damaged merchandise. But
if I'd known the bear was going to be killed
I wouldn't have called anyone. I would have just waited
for him to walk out of the store.

My son's very upset. He fought so hard, he says. And
the choke was on too long.

He could have torn us apart, he was so strong, one of the Fish
& Game men tells me.

Bear removal is out of our jurisdiction, says the
    Forest Service.

Redacted from Taos News, August 28, 1981

GRRRRR

The Year the Bears Invaded Duluth

They must have descended from the night sky,
Ursa Major emptied,
whipped in on the winds of space.
Or maybe across the frozen straits
from the Steppes,
lean and hungry,
the winter having been too long.

They swarmed the dumps,
pawing through the spoiled and fetid leavings,
raided root cellars,
lumbered like scraggly drunks
through all the best neighborhoods.

When I rode with Grandpa to town,
we'd see at least three
bears treed, the crowds below
circling like dogs
ready to close in for the kill,
keeping them there
to wait for the bear truck.

Sometimes four or five would wade
slow, as if grass were water,
into our orchard,
would rear up to take the green apples
sour juice dripping,
narrow eyes squeezed a little in pleasure.
Oh, it was good, you could tell,
and they kept returning
despite Uncle Odd
who ran like an avenger up the hill
with his rifle firing wildly.

One sleepy morning a bear
walked bold as berries
through the revolving door
of the Hotel Duluth.

continued on next page

Imagine his consternation:
people like a flock of startled birds
except the one man reading the paper
who heard nothing.

By the time a small one wandered
into our blacksmith shop
I'd gotten used to them.
Uncle Gunnar shut the door
and called the game warden.
I pressed my nose to the window
to see the bear, he pressed his
next to mine: two pointy noses,
four curious eyes.

If angry uncle hadn't swept me up,
would he have broken that pane,
reached for me?

I never thought so.
He seemed as curious as I.
So out of his element
he thought perhaps he was dreaming
of a ghost girl falling
into the well of his eyes
or the surprise smell
of iron and rust, old harness,
the acrid bite of coal dust
that puffed like powder
with each shuffling step.

By winter they were gone.
The apples they had left uneaten
were mounded and cidery
in our root cellar.
The bears of the north sky remained
bright and mythic, predictable
as the snow that swept to the roofs
of the houses below.

J. R. Brady

From

Merging Traffic

I read that, in Los Angeles,
an elderly bear was found
soaking in a suburb hot tub.
A photo shows him passive,
sitting sedated in a cage
while officials seek a zoo.
He can't survive on his own
anymore. His teeth are broken
from foraging in garbage cans.

Jnana Hodson

Primer for Bear

shining lake
of running bruin

his laughing stream

brown belly
full of huckleberry
—his women pregnant

YAH-KUH-MAH

guarding homes
throughout the valley
that bears his name

David Meuel

Grizzly

(Glacier National Park, Montana)

He could kill me with a swat,
that rolling mass of fur and meat and bone
who owns the meadow just below. And,
if his belly told him to,
he'd chew me up and wash me down
with twenty-thousand huckleberries
and absolutely
no regrets.

Bear Poison

Even from the back seat of the Buick,
the boy feels the impact.
His father steps out of their car
with dreamy slowness
and the boy follows, ignoring his mother's
Get back here young man.
Father swears in the stage lights of the sedan.
The rain pulses through its low beams.
The wipers, waiting for him
to lug the carcass of a bear cub off the hood,
groan free along the fractured windshield.
The body is close enough to touch,
the eyes cup a dull cosmos, the tongue lolls,
nostrils ooze like broken honeycomb.

Searching their cabinets at home that night,
the boy forages among the dentures
worn down to the pink
and fine-toothed combs clotted with hair
for Aqua Velva and cough syrup
to fill his old fishbowl.
He'll leave his mother's nicotine gum
stiffening inside its tinfoil.
Hair cream worms from its tube.
Nothing to hurt the bears
just to intoxicate, to domesticate.
Maybe they'll forget their nature,
maybe they'll stay with him forever.

Soon this boy awakens to a breath
rising and falling with his own
and lifts his shade for a circus
of hulking shadows drawn to the bait.
The smallest, snuffling around his window,
nose-prints the glass with wet marks
shaped like infinity from math class,
and still this boy is unafraid
of the dim universe in its eyes.

He tries to open the window
shut tight as gristle around bone.
They wait for him under a flat-stone moon
and rasp their backs against his home.
He struggles for what seems a lifetime.

Beyond the calm glass, wind voices its hunger,
and the pack returns to their thicket,
but the small one looks back and licks
the boy's concoction from its muzzle
as if to remember his sweetness.

When Spring Came and the Blue Bear Came to Town

When the blue bear came to town,
we played our saxophone.
Listening, it shook its head in salmonberry bushes,
pushed and rooted in the earth.
It came each night, at dusk,
to Gastineau – the avenue at the edge –
to our dumpsters, porches, and steps
sagging with rain.
We played, we sang, we clapped our hands,
hoping it would cross to us;
but it came only as far as our garbage,
then turned back. We, too, returned home,
speaking of the wildness of it,
the blueness of it – like glaciers, like denim.
We could not find the words.
We followed, each night, as far as we dared,
with our saxophone, with our French horn –
a line of minstrels bound to a cave
through a wood of ancient spruce
wild as cellos not yet carved.

Fellow Travelers

Out of low popple woods
a little fellow came,
August-ridden,
to lay his head
against our garbage can
and fall asleep;
he didn't even eat.
My mother, seeing him,
went bravely forth,
armed only with the pot
she beat, woke
the little fellow up
and moved him smartly out;
sometimes I think of this
when I can't sleep.

And later,
on a rising trail
through sterner country
where the real ones ruled,
we laughed, we swore
and sang and yelled,
we moved them smartly out,
one summer's trail crew
coming through . . .
But we'd be quiet as,
at a low spot in the trail,
we watched the water gather
in a track; the claws
at least
would not retract.

Yet there was another trail
that didn't climb or cross
— through open lodgepole,
a sunlit, easy walk.
And once, all by myself,
someone fell in behind me,

continued on next page

about my size but wider.
We were that way awhile,
easy going, going easy,
as if he were just out walking
his own pale ghost
on a long ghost leash.
Until, at some right point,
he veered to amble cross-country,
on the track of his nose
to where – I'm sure –
the keenest of the sweets
were hid.

Walking the Geography of Other Nations

At the outlet of the river, where water runs cool and fresh into salt,
its muscle flattens into a low run at the waves,
like a single wolf will run crouched
and come in under the belly of danger.

We walked the littoral of Oliver Lagoon,
mud like black bean soup up our shins
and it sucked at our boots, possessing.

The forest was quiet: skunk cabbage and devil's club
their huge leaves like a giant's garden,
one armed with odor, the other with thorns.

We followed bear paths, reading their stories:
here the cloven < < < of a deer going fast,
there a scatter of bones, then the flat shovel-dent
of bull moose, his velvet caught on the hemlock's torn bark.

Ho, Bear, we shouted as we walked his realm
stepping over evidence of fox and our first bear scat,
old now and dried into a tidy bundle of feathers.
And then – large paw prints. Something was coming in
under our bellies, something was a shadow in the spruce.

And rounding an elbow of path – green, wet, fresh,
bear scat still warm. The woods were full of eyes.
Ho, Bear we called again, this time in homage, in surrender
as we retraced our steps, yielding the forest.

The 59th Bear

We counted bears – as if all we wanted
Were more bears. Yellowstone
Folded us into its robe, its tepees
Of mountain and conifer.
Mislaid Red Indian Mickey Mouse America
Pointered us from campground to campground –
We were two of many. And it was as novel-astonishing
To you as to me. Paradise, we saw,
Was where wild bears ate from the hands of children.
Were these real wild bears? We saw Daddies
Supporting their babies piggyback on dark bears
In a dancing ring of guffaws and cameras.
The bears were in on the all-American family.
Originals of those board cut-out bears,
Uncle Bruins in Disneyland overalls,
Who warned against forest fires. Bears waited –
Welcoming committees – at every parking,
Lifting their teddybear ears and quizzing buttons
At the car windows. Twenty, we counted.
Thirty. Forty. Fifty. Once
As I opened the car door at a café
A bear that just happened to be passing
Shouldered it shut.
Everywhere people were entertaining
Bears and bears were entertaining people.

We roamed, soon at home in the marvellous abundance.
Eagles were laid on too. We leaned at a rail
And looked down onto floating black flecks
That turned out to be eagles – we were swept
Into the general exclamatory joy
By somebody's binoculars. I stared
Down through the spread fingers of an eagle
Into a drop that still scares me to remember.
But it all refused to be translated.
The Camp Ranger notices seemed perfunctory,
Make-believe. Through coy nicknames magma
Bubbled its colours, belched its labouring sighs –

Prehistory was still at boiling point,
Smoking round us.
                              Each evening
Bears raided the campgrounds. Camera stars,
They performed at the sunken trash-bins. Delight —
Every few days a whole new class of campers
Squealing for fearless close-ups before
The warnings sank in.
                              Somehow that night
The warnings had sunk in. You were nervous.
It had been a day of worsening nerves.
We had driven just too far. The gas
Had got too low and the evening too late.

Your spirits as usual had gone right down with
The fuel-gauge to the bottom, and bobbed there —
You saw us in a vision, a headline,
Devoured in the night-woods. One curve in the road
Became dreadful — nearly impassable.
A giant elk detached itself abruptly
From the conifer black, wheeled its rigging
Right above the bonnet and vanished, like a sign
From some place of omens. We reached our tent
 In the dusk of campfires.
                              Three cold fried trout
Were surplus from breakfast. But
It was too late to sit up under the stars
Sipping eating — "The bears!" The bears were coming!
With a racket of clatter-pans, and a yelling
From the far end of the campground — Bears! Bears!' —
You panicked into the tent and pleaded.
I saw a big brown bear and a smaller, darker,
Romping like big rubber toys,
Bouncing along, like jolly inflatables
Among the tents and tables. Awesome, fluid,
Unpredictable, dodging swiftness! And cries.
The whole campground was jumpy — a cacophony
Of bangings and shouts urging the bears
On and away elsewhere — anywhere away
Pestering somebody else. I locked everything

continued on next page

Into the car. Each thing carefully checked.
One thing I missed.
                              Did we sleep?
The campground slept. The bears had been scared off,
To other campgrounds. How safe we felt
In our green breathing walls! Hidden breathers,
Safe and chrysalis in our sleeping bags,
Trusting each moment to elide into another
As quiet as itself. Vast, bristling darkness
Of America. Under my pillow –
Drastic resource for a drastic emergency –
I kept the hatchet, purposefully sharpened.

What time was it? A rending crash – too close –
Had me head up and alert, listening,
As if I watched what made it. Then more rendings
Of real awful damage going on,
Still being done – and you were awake too,
Listening beside me. I got up
And peered through the tent's window mesh into moonlight.
Everything clear, black-shadowed. The car
Five paces away, looked natural enough.
Then more rippings inside it, and it shook.
And I saw the dark blockage, a black mass
Filling the far rear window. 'Those damned bears!
One's getting into the car.'
                              A few shock-shouts,
I thought, a close-up assault of human abuse,
And the bear would be off. I'd take my hatchet
Just in case. I got out my hatchet,
Pitifully unimaginative.
I was remembering those amiable bears.
That's how it happens. Your terrors
Were more intelligent, with their vision –
And I was not so sure. Then for an hour
He was unpacking the car, unpuzzling our bags,
Raking and thumping. I imagined
Every scrap of fabric ripped from the springs.
It sounded like a demolition. We lay
Decoding every variety of sound

As he battered and squelched, crunched and scraped
With still intervals of meditation.
I got up again. In first faint light
I made him out wrestling our steel freezer
Between his paws. 'It's the big brown one.' We'd heard
He was the nasty one. Again we lay quiet,
Letting him do what he wanted.
                                        And at last
A new sound — the caress, ushering closer,
The lullaby reveille of a cruising engine:
The Camp Ranger's car, doing the dawn rounds.
The bear heard it. And we had the joy —
Awful incredulity like joy —
Of hearing his claw-bunches hurry-scuffle
To the secret side of our tent. He was actually there,
Hiding beside our tent! His breathing,
Heavy after the night's gourmandizing,
Rasped close to the canvas — only inches
From your face that, big-eyed, stared at me
Staring at you.
              The car cruised easily away
Into the forest and lake silence. The bear
Faded from his place, as the tent walls paled.
Loons on the glassed lake shook off their nightmares.
The day came.
              A ghoul had left us,
Leaving our freezer buckled open, our fish
Vanished from their stains, every orange
Sucked flat, our pancake mix
Dabbled over yards of dust, everything
Edible gone, in a scatter of wrappers
And burst cartons. And the off rear window of the car
Wrenched out — a star of shatter splayed
From a single talon's leverage hold,
A single claw forced into the hair-breadth odour
Had ripped the whole sheet out. He'd leaned in
And on claw hooks lifted out our larder.
He'd left matted hairs. I glued them in my Shakespeare.

continued on next page

I felt slightly dazed – a strange pride
To have been so chosen and ego-raked
By the deliberations of that beast.

But you came back from the wash-house
With your last-night's panic double-boosted
For instant flight.
                              Some doppelgänger,
That very night, at the next campground,
Had come out of his tent to shoo off a bear
With a torch and a few shouts. He'd learned –
Briefly, in what flash of reckoning
He'd been allowed – what I had hardly guessed:
A bear's talons, which by human flesh
Can be considered steel, braced on tendons
Of steel hawser, are on the end of an arm
That can weigh sixty, seventy, eighty pounds
Moving at 90 m.p.h.
Your terror had the mathematics perfect.
You had met a woman in the wash-house
Who'd driven terrified from that other campground.
And you just knew, it was that very same bear.
Having murdered a man, he'd romped through the woods
To rob us.
That was our fifty-ninth bear. I saw, well enough,
The peril that see-saws opposite
A curious impulse – what slight flicker
In a beast's brain electrifies tonnage
And turns life to paper. I did not see
What flicker in yours, what need later
Transformed our dud scenario into a fiction –
Or what self-salvation
Squeezed the possible blood out of it
Through your typewriter ribbon.
                              At that time
I had not understood
How the death hurtling to and fro
Inside your head, had to alight somewhere
And again somewhere, and had to be kept moving,
And had to be rested
Temporarily somewhere.

Bob and the Bear

Bob drove his jeep and trailer to the ledge
About four. The sun slid south on its way
Down behind Dragonback. The warm fall day
Was on its way to frost. Bob, on the edge
Of the loglanding, backed to the logfall,
To the fir culls that lined the drainage ditch.
Hard against the hillside he cut the switch,
Set the brakes, manhandled his splitting maul,
Bucking saw, gascan, wedges, from the back.
He set saw choke, jerked the rope to set saw
Choking on raw gas and oil. He set raw
Sound to bounce off the mountainside and stack
Itself like cordwood in the trembling air.
Raw chips spewed like those raw sounds. Rounds tumbled
Behind the trailer. Bob rested, grumbled,
Drained his canteen, looked up to see a bear,
Eyes like mean marbles, muzzle full of teeth
And salt slaver. He jumped for the jeep, slammed
Himself inside. The bear waddled, stood, crammed
His claws into whatever lay beneath
The cab and rocked. Bob swore. He had no gun.
Behind the trailer lay his saw, his wood,
Blocking backing. Void gaped before his hood.
He honked. The bear bashed his paw hard on one
Window. Bob honked again. The black bear scowled
And snuffled, snorted, stood and glared at him.
Bob stayed in, the bear out, the light grew dim,
Dusky. It was dark before the bear growled,
Grunted, left the landing. Bob threw the cut
Wood in the ditch, backed the trailer out, cursed,
Drove down the mountain, swore still as he nursed
His beer that weekend, bears would regret what
Bears had done. They didn't. Nor did Bob who
Told everybody what I just told you.

Mythos

She rends the night with yellow claws, wails for her cub,
long dead, pierced in its tiny heart by the devil's arrow,
now red-tipped and still.

She ran the devil up a tree, not bowing to vengeance but to grief.
They found the cub cradled in a shallow near Nether Valley.
He was never found, although they never really looked.

He was from Galesville, his father a farmer and his mother a bundle of regret.
Folks predicted he'd end badly; some celebrated his death at Boone's,
raised brimming glasses of corn liquor to a bear soon to be legend.

He ate warm chicken hearts as a child, later drove the tractor off Casey's Ledge,
wore his mother's slips (this was, above all, her greatest regret).
He vowed to kill his father, the preacher, the whole town on his 16th birthday.

She found him hunched over the cub, they say, fist-fighting through swampy flesh
        for its heart
until she severed his spine with one slap;
only then did he drop the bow his father had carved from the hickory tree out back.

She dragged the cub to the place of its birth just a short time before,
followed the sun-dappled trail west to a creek-carved shallow,
far from where the devil shivered in the upper branches of an oak.

He set fire to the O'Connell's fields, spooked Clayson's bull into an unforgiving
        hailstorm
and cracked a hole through the crusted ice on Yeoman's Pond to drown a colt.
For this, and much more, the preacher offered an exorcism at no cost to his parents.

He took to the idea of an exorcism much as the yearling took to the freezing water.
He bolted after breaking church windows, casting rocks wrapped in misspelled
        notes
promising within the year death to his father, the townsfolk, the exorcist.

She moved with the sun as it arced westward, and she stopped to rest
just as the boy, who had scrambled down the tree, met with a band of gypsies
who slit his throat on the Freedom Trail.

She could not have divined, or cared, that fear of finding the boy alive
would prevent folks from looking, would cause them instead to painstakingly
water a myth blossomed neatly from a hickory arrow lodged in the chest of a
ravaged cub.

Grizzly

Summer-ranger said they half-fell
from that goddamned jackpine
like bad fruit.
Said he watched them pick through the damp cloth.

They told me they had left
the trail.
Had woke that night
to his snuffling.
Fought out of their bags
and climbed.

Said they had pressed their faces
bloody against the bark
trying not to hear her voice

"It's eating me."

And one said how happy
he was when that stopped.

Treat Each Bear As The Last Bear

THE BLIND BOY and his mother were terrified when they heard a polar bear outside their tiny house. They knew that it could smash into the house and eat them, so the mother handed the boy his bow and arrow and helped him notch an arrow. Because she was too weak to pull back the bow, and since he was blind, the mother had to tell her son where to aim. When he killed the bear, that greedy mother lied to her son telling him that he had missed. She went outside and hid the polar bear meat for herself, cooking a little bit whenever she was hungry.

—from an Inūpiaq myth

The Bear on Main Street

What made the man kill this bear?
His truck, across which the bear's body lies,
tells me it wasn't to feed his family
or because his children were cold,
at least not for lack of fur.

The bear has beautiful black feet, delicate
almost, like the soles of patent leather slippers,
and the wind riffles the surface of its fur
with the sheen of water in the autumn sun.

The bear looks as if it might only be sleeping,
but its tongue lags from its mouth, and the man
has wrapped it with stout twine and bound it
to the bed of his truck,
as if he were afraid it might speak.

Three teenage boys pull their pickup to the curb.
One of the boys guesses what the bear must weigh.
Another wants to know how many shots it took,
and the third boy climbs down. He strokes its nose and forehead.
He traces the bear's no longer living skull
with the living bones of his fingers
and wonders by what impossible road
he will come to his father's country.

No Bear But One

High above the ordered villages
among the serpentine and cypress
under the voiceless stars
we meet. Night after night
he sits, huge pawed,
shagged and bearded with extinction.
I pass through his embrace
soft and close as mist,
tread the twisting ridges,
night after night,
hair whitening,
but not toward dawn.

PHIL FRANK

The Pledge of the California Bear

for the grizzled silvertip
who now treads
only the red-starred rectangle
of the state flag
and the concrete grottoes
of our gloomy zoos

and to the children
    of Lakeshore School,
for whom I offer this prayer
every morning
(over the drone of that other pledge)
as the bear flag flaps,
and patiently waits
beneath Old Glory's tired stripes

"I pledge attention
To the Bear
Of my heart's nocturnal forests,
And to the fescue
On which it stands,
One spirit,
Which is God,
Masquerading,
With tooth and claw
And soft belly for all.

Margaret's Trophy

Polar bear, you're the taxidermist's
dream: mouth propped open
in a snarl, legs arranged as if to
lunge from fake tundra in the gun store.
A window display of a silenced beast
with heart and lungs gone,
stuffed like a child's toy.

A metal plaque proclaims
a woman named Margaret shot you
at Point Hope, Alaska.

As a cub you slept in a den, learned
to lope over snow, fish a meal
from ice. Your body grew strong,
fat layered bone, you drifted
miles on ice floes in a robe
of warm hair, a solitary shadow
on the white landscape, reduced now
to a dead-yellow fur coat in civilization,
a California shopping center.

Across the walls guns are mounted:
heavy rifles to rip flesh, to blind,
to find the brain that remembers
birth, and knows trails to food,
that recalls the song of the walrus —
until the blizzard of pain
comes, blood erupting on the snow,
your dark claws releasing
the frozen land where
the sun-starved days were ending
and spring was waking.

The Bear

The hostess drapes a snowy hand,
its nails maroon, over her conversation piece,
the six-foot polar bear beside the couch.
A press of human bodies steams
the sealed-up drawing room. They toast the north,
pipeline and tanker running in the black.
Then conversations crack apart
and one by one the guests begin to float
over to him, his seams impeccable,
blue satin bow to match wainscot and swag.
Some make sport of sitting in his lap.
Some lend him pipe and tie.
Some stroke the artful plush,
tracing the welt of his embroidered grin.

Only the small daughter, on parade
in blue-sashed pinafore, shies,
screws her dollface up into a howl.
She is swept off to bed, the incident
blotted like spilt champagne.
Denned upstairs in her crib, she hears
the party rumble and chink, makes of it
stars rattling like ice,
plucked cube by cube from a black bucket.
Sinking asleep, she dreams translucent blue
caverns and crags. A lunge; a stun of paw.
A steaming seal, its split red belly.
Waking, she cries above the revelers
and will not be consoled.

Down Home Cooking

It's not surprising mama was ample.
She cooked crisp-skin chicken
that melted down your chin,
goose with gooseberry sauce,
juicy free-range beef,
and fermented chokecherry wine
in great crocks
behind the wood stove.

On baking day, little tendrils of scent
tugged you from the best games
to hand-churned butter
over crunchy loaves,
cinnamon twists, caramel nut rolls
and chocolate chip cookies
warm as a fat lap.

Towards the end of winter
we tired of our root-crop and apples
molding toward slime in the cellar.
Home-canned vegetables looked
bleached as old bones in bottles.
Even mama's magic
couldn't make new what was too old.
We wanted meat and found it,
when lucky, deep in the woods.

Once, Uncle Gunnar went hunting
in the upper 40. He was looking
for deer or moose. He found bear,
an angry early riser,
snow still quilting his lair.

Mama was an alchemist with game,
reasoned bear was the same.
She cut it into steaks.
The whole house smelled
of good meat cooking.

She and Gunnar grinned,
said nothing as we ate
around the big trestle table.

After Uncle Odd said, "delicious"
and again "delicious,"
and then once more –
which was one time too many –
Gunnar just had to tell him "bear".
"Bear!" yelled Odd,
rearing up, knocking over his chair.

Ursine on hind legs,
the enormous rug
of his chest, claws,
the powerful jaws –
as if to become
what was taboo to eat.

Unlike Odd, we ate that meat
for more than a week,
laughed at foolish Uncle
who let his head
get in the way of his stomach.

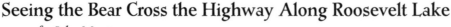
Seeing the Bear Cross the Highway Along Roosevelt Lake

—for John Mercier

I.
He is small, very black;
moves fast . . .

What made him cross the busy highway?
Where was he going as we hurried to Inchelium?

Below is the dam that holds back,
in the Grand Coulee, the Columbia

creating this lake of motorboats and water skiers.
Hin-Mah-Too-Yah-Lat-Kekt wonders why

the picnic tables?
Who stopped the river mightier than the wind

that brings its message down from Canada?
Are the *coho* and *chinook* still down there
in the depths of the buried river?

II.
Along the road to Nespelem
a man sells wind dried salmon
from his station wagon.

The sign in the agency offices
say *"Lim Lim* For Not Smoking."

The tribal forester explains:
Lim Lim means 'Thank You" in Colville.

There's trouble here in this small world:
ennui and suicide, white man's words.

But off to the west where the asphalt road ends,
in the timber of rising mountains,
are the sacred grounds of the forgotten.

A Black Bear

A black bear hangs
from a branch
by a rope attached
to a meat hook

in the back
of his skull,

chest split open
like a cunt
in *Hustler,*

rear paws
craving
our blood-
pocked earth,

eyes upraised
to an autumn sky
that has forsaken him.

Bear News

A female bear, lactating,
teats still filled with milk,
was killed by a truck on Route 9
near Cummington, Massachusetts,
where you can still hear
sounds of fife and drum
and weeping captives
in the breeze ruffling
the tops of the oaks
and the maples,
and the tops of King George's
straight and tall white pines.
A guy I met told me
he drove up about five minutes
after the incident,
saw half a dozen cars near the spot.
"I thought
it was a speed trap," he said,
"until I slowed down and saw
the bear there,
still warm.
We looked for the cubs,
but they were nowhere around,
probably old enough to survive
without her,
but you wonder
if they have the smarts.
Yeah, I got there
about five minutes
after she got hit.
Body still warm.
Not a mark on her.
Shiny fur."
Maybe the cubs will be fine.
The blueberries and blackberries
are plentiful this year.
Plenty to eat.
Rest in peace.

I shot that bear and left it
for a week, come back, the damn bear
was all bloated up.
I built a raft, took it to the center of the lake,
tied two big rocks to the damn bear's feet,
pushed him overboard.
Goddamn bear don't sink.
Too full of gas he
ain't been dressed out. I'll fix that, so I
come along side him in my canoe, start to cut
with my knife. Well, gas and guts and grease
come roaring out of that hole, knocks me
out of the canoe, covered.
the damn bear sinks.
two months later it's the best fishing
in the whole damn lake.
they come to get the worms
feeding on that bear,
and the place has been called
"Bear Hole" ever since.

Bear Bait

Any sack of rotting meat will do.
A net bag of butcher scraps hanging in a tree,
offal from another kill. The stench of meat
brings bears. And so, as is the custom here,
a hunting guide paid glue factory price
for a coal black mare off the reservation.

Too fat to work, too small to ride
she was corralled alone for the night.
In the morning he would load her with supplies,
tie her into his string of pack horses,
lead her into the mountains to a blind,
shoot her in the head, and hang her carcass.

I do not sleep in bear country, listening
through nylon walls to the skitterings
of small rodents. In the nightly chase
of hunter and bears filling the northern sky,
pursuer and prey pivot around the lodestar
pulling night to day, winter to spring.

Dream bears rise at dusk from day beds
of duff and bear grass, bodies lean
and high humped, long-skulled faces, peering
close-set eyes yellow for the charge.
Facing bears I cannot see, I wear curved claws
for courage, a bear bone at my throat.

We tread in common footprints, in downfall
and windfall, through lodgepole and ash.
Grizzled hair lifted and rigid
we stand upright, squinting,
sniffing, listening in the oldest fear
of he who fears nothing. Who is here?

At sunrise, in a shed at the end
of the empty corral, the hunting guide
found the mare lying on the ground,

beside her a black foal with spotted coat
of white starred appaloosa magic.
He quit using horses to bait bears.

He did not stop baiting bears from blinds
for men to hang the heads and hides on trophy walls.
Winter sleepers, fur men, ice bears too hungry
in the night of early spring, rogue bears,
boss bears, she bears, when bears hunt men
any sack of rotting meat will do.

The Man

See, a small space in the woods,
green overgrown with green,
shadows trees brush entangled
At the edge of the clearing a man
a white man, middle-aged, aging
just his face stands out in the dimness
"dominion over every living thing"
a hunter's jacket, hunter's cap
He lifts the spear of his rifle barrel
aims
with cold, hard, arthritic hands
16 years on the line, finally made foreman,
finally inspector, finally retired
The cold, square, aging jaws of the man
are barely flushed, a tingle of fear
or pleasure as he aims

diagonally across the clearing
into the black furry mass of the bear
She sits on her haunches, back to a stump,
an ancient, massive, dog-nosed brute
pawing the dogs
who yap & skitter away
(My mother's mother, huge in her dress,
sits in the creeks, swatting the water & laughing)
She is warm, stupid, she smells of bear
an abundance of flesh, stumpy limbs,
stone of a head & little pig eyes
teats where she rears, in the black close fur
She smells like my mother/my mother's mother
she does not understand
she won't get away

The man with the rifle aiming
confers with the other shadowy men
ranging the edge of the clearing
Each in position: they have agreed

which one will have her/whose turn it is
One of them covers the kill

My mother does not understand
rears, paws, shakes her head & its wattles of fur
thinking she's won

Afterwards the body is hoisted
"a sack full of lard" on inaccurate scales
is hung, dressed, weighed on accurate scales
The skull (unshattered, unhurt) is found eligible
for Boone & Crockett official measuring
The head is stuffed & mounted
                              safe on the walls
where every evening he enters, approaches
fires recoils fires into the small stupid eyes
"the thrill of a lifetime" my mother

Well

Well the house cats were always sleeping
And the goats spent days inventing holes in the fence
And the bear came down only as far as the hives
And knocked their rocks off and scattered the sweet frames

Well the cats wandered to the screen door and complained
In unison and when I opened it decided not to
And the goats got up on top of each other no matter which kind
And the bear froze in the sheriff's searchlight

Well the cats set out within days of the U-Haul
And the son disappeared but the mother somehow found us
And the goats belongs to no one not then not ever
And the bear fell heavily to the ground and it took a winch

last black bear of the upper peninsula speaks

you took thirty
of my kind last season, their hides adorning
knotty pine basement dens, hearts fare for
wolves, coyotes,

but beware,
soon mattress springs will rust in roadside dust,
kennel dogs waxen fat, guns lose oily hues, c.b.s
and four-wheel hubs no longer hum, hunting seasons
wasted at rural taverns, baits rotting at home,

send me
a last woodsman with provisions and knife, only
arrows to target, one pure redshirt with single
cartridge,

let the final hunt be fair.

*The richest, most diversified grizzly bear habitats were found
in the state of California . . . . The only incontestable fact
about California grizzly bears is that there aren't any left.
We shot them all.*

Doug Peacock

*The fate of bears in many areas of the world will be decided
in the next 10–20 years. The future of several species is in
serious doubt. The elimination of bears from 50–75 percent
of their historic range has already occurred and the
remaining range will decrease unless serious efforts are
focused on bear conservation.*

Dr. Chris Servheen

Treat each bear as the last bear.

Each wolf the last, each caribou.

Each track the last track.

Gone spoor, gone scat.

There are no more deertrails,

no more flyways.

Treat each animal as sacred,

each minute our last.

Ghost hooves. Ghost skulls.

Death rattles and

dry bones.

Each bear walking alone

in warm night air.

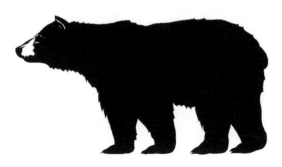

Hannah Ackerman: *I miss the good old days when the Los Angeles City Zoo was at its former small site and admission was free. A kid could visit the bears as often as she wanted and senior discounts were unnecessary.* Ackerman teaches English and hikes the San Gabriels. In the Sierra a bear once tried, persistently, to share breakfast. She has won awards and appeared in many magazines, such as *Albatross, Poetry, Cumberland Poetry Review, New Zoo Poetry Review.* She lives in California.

Gail Aggen: *My interest in bears came through my husband's quest for meaning. He dreams of bears every so often. Maybe the brown bear identifies the substance of his 'geist.' Maybe the bear is an alien presence or maybe the brown bear is me.* Aggen is both poet and painter. Her published poems and her art shows are many. She lives in Missouri.

Bettina T. Barrett: *Bear – the grizzly – is a most important presence in my life.* Barrett was born and grew up in Denmark and came to the United States at age 15. She draws, paints, and *plays* in clay where bears often enter. She has published *Bear-Star My Name* and *Sleepdancer.* She lives in California.

Richard Beban: *I was, in fact, a "Mission Bear" – a graduate of Mission High School in San Francisco – but my affinity for the species goes even farther back to a number of stuffed pandas I had as a child, one of whom met an end so gruesome I hesitate to even try to explore it poetically.* He lives in California.

Sandia Belgrade (Sbear): is a bear with Jewish and lesbian roots. She was part of the Women's Internet Project which gave a panel presentation and provided computer training at the United Nations World Conference on Women in Beijing. She is an editorial consultant, has written an opera libretto working its way toward production and is the author of books, including: *At the Sweet Hour of Hand in Hand* and *Children of the Second Birth,* and has in progress, *In Search of the Lodestar* (novel) and *The Spirit Avoiding Capture* (poetry). She lives in California.

Mary H. Ber: *This poem is an entity in itself. However, it was composed according to the imagery in a dream I had shortly after my husband's death, when I was deep in grief. Since our last name is pronounced 'bear' and is derived from the animal's name, the symbolism is obvious.* Ber teaches English at Roosevelt University, publishes and edits *Moon Journal,* a literary magazine, and is completing a Master's Degree in Women's Studies. She has published short stories, poems, and essays. She lives in Illinois.

Pam Bernard: *One of the safe places I seek during meditation is on the lap of a bear the size of a small room.* Bernard, a poet and painter, holds a BA from Harvard University and her MFA in Creative Writing from the Program for Writers at Warren Wilson College. In 1998 she received a Fellowship in Poetry from the Massachusetts Cultural Council and an NEA Fellowship in Creative Writing. She lives in Massachusetts.

DC Berry: *A bear ate the lit birthday cake of a neighboring camper, and on another camping trip, my wife thought a bear was in the tent next door. Was a guy snoring.* Berry's publications include *Divorce Boxing,* 1998, *Jawbone,* 1978 and *Saigon Cemetery,* 1972. His poems have appeared in such magazines as *Poetry* and *Chicago Review.* He lives in Mississippi.

William Borden: *"Bear Warning" derives from a morning on a lake in Minnesota many years ago. My son, then 12, recently confessed that he was the perpetrator of the paw prints. A few years ago I joined a bear researcher in northern Minnesota for a day and hung out with two radio-collar black bears.* Borden is Chester Fritz Distinguished Professor of English Emeritus at The University of North Dakota, Fiction Editor of *The North Dakota Quarterly,* and a member of The Dramatists Guild and PEN. His short stories and poems have appeared in many anthologies and magazines. *Superstoe,* a novel, has been published successively by Victor Gollancz, Harper & Row and recently by Orloff Press. *Slow Step and Dance* (poems) appeared in 1991. He lives in Minnesota.

Allen Braden: *Not too long ago, my young nephew Zach called for the bear poison recipe in order to tame the wild things living nearby, not just grizzlies but for the neighborhood cats and his big sister too.* Braden received the Grolier Poetry Prize and an Artist Trust grant in 1998. He lives in Washington.

J. R. Brady: *I was fond of a small brown bear named Maud, who once lived at the San Francisco Zoo. She loved attention and would put on quite a show. It seemed to me, even as a city kid, that a bear shouldn't have to live that way. I always felt she was making the best of a bad situation and whenever I thought of her I would imagine her standing by a waterfall deep in some long vanished forest.* Brady is an actor, playwright and poet. Her plays have been presented in the United States and Scotland. Her most recent play, Loch Ness, was produced in 1997 and 1999. Poetry collections include: *Generations, Merging Traffic* and *Vanished Laughter*. She has recorded her poetry in collaboration with musician, Jon Greene, and she is included in a 1999 CD, *Alchemy of the Word*. She lives in California.

Barbara Brent Brower: *My Ojibway friends tell me the bear is my spirit guide and I wanted to see a live one. Of the bear in the poem, I have the skull and front claws and photographs of his body as it lay in the grass. A week later, a live bear walked out of the forest, stood up and waved.* Brower's bear poem won the Grand Prize in the Arizona Poetry Society competition. She has received the Brodine Prize and was second in the Vickers Competition. Her work appears in many journals among them *Snowy Egret, Connecticut River Review* and *Great River Review*. She lives in Michigan.

Grace Butcher: *My house is full of bears. I lost Big Teddy on a train ride when I was 6; I think I've been replacing him ever since.* Butcher is a retired English professor from Kent State University, where she also founded and coached the running program. Her recent book, *Child, House, World*, won the Ohio Poet of the Year Award in 1991. She has also written *Rumors of Ecstasy . . . Rumors of Death* and *Before I go Out on the Road*. She competes nationally in track events, and has been both champion, and record holder. She is also an avid motorcyclist, camping, racing motocross and road racing.

Hayden Carruth has published twenty-two books of poetry, a novel, four books of criticism and two anthologies. He has been editor of *Poetry, Harpers,* and advisory editor of the *Hudson Review*. He has received grants from the Guggenheim Foundation, Bollingen Foundation, the NEA, a Lannan Literary Fellowship, and won the Lenore Marshall/Nation Prize, Ruth Lilly Poetry Prize and several others. He won the 1996 National Book Award for *Scrambled Eggs & Whiskey*. Other books include: *Nothing for Tigers, The Crow and the Heart, From Snow and Rock, from Chaos* and his latest, *Reluctantly: Autobiographical Essays,* 1998. He lives in upstate New York.

Robert M. Chute is a poet and a biologist, whose segment of poem used here is from his chapbook *When Grandmother Decides to Die,* two poems from the tradition of the Abenaki nation of the Kennebecs. Though the Abenaki were among the first native peoples of North America to encounter the Europeans, their history and culture are unknown to most contemporary Americans. Chute teaches at Bates College. He has authored essays, papers on parasites in hibernating mammals, a biology textbook, and environmental essays. His poems and stories have appeared in many journals and he is the author of *Thirteen Moons, Woodshed on the Moon: Thoreau Poems, Androscoggin Too,* and others. He lives in Maine.

Jim White Bear Cody is a poet, essayist, prose writer, registered nurse and teacher. He is the author of *Colorado River, Return, Prayer to Fish, A Book of Wonders, My Body Is A Flute,* and the forthcoming *Elvis, Immortality, and Other Poems*. He has taught English in Korea, translated Old Gaelic and Spanish and is currently continuing his doctoral studies of post-colonial literature. *When I was a young poet, I wrote deliberate poems about the bear. It is said, in some cultures, that when a human focuses on one particular animal, admires it, imitates it, that animal favors the human. So occasionally I seek out bears and am blessed with a poem or two.* He and his Korean wife have a small daughter who goes *unnnnh* when she is angry, as she is bear by lineage. In the year 2,333 B.C.E., the Son of Heaven came down to earth because he wished to be a human being. He met a bear woman and a tiger, also wishing to be human. The Son of Heaven told them they must each go live in a cave and eat nothing but garlic for 100 days. The one to survive would be allowed to become human. The bear woman won and married the Son of Heaven. Their first offspring was Dan Guen, the first Korean king, from whom all Koreans are descended. The Codys live in Washington.

SuzAnne C. Cole: *The bear as a symbol of healing is important to me, figuring prominently in dreams and trances. I collect bear fetishes and carry a tiny jade bear on all my travels.* Cole, a former college English instructor, is author of *To Our Heart's Content: Meditations for Women Turning 50.* Her work has appeared in *Newsweek, the Houston Chronicle, Bless the Day, There's No Place Like Home for the Holidays,* and such literary magazines as *Potpourri, Rag Mag, Mind Matters Review, Lynx, RiverSedge,* and *Maverick Press.* She lives in Texas.

Billy Collins is author of five books of poetry, including *The Art of Drowning, Questions and Angels* (selected for the National Poetry Series,) and *Picnic, Lightning.* His poetry has appeared in such periodicals as *Poetry, American Poetry Review, American Scholar, Harper's, Paris Review,* and *The New Yorker.* He has won fellowships from the NY Foundation, NEA, and Guggenheim, and has received prizes such as the Bess Hoskin, Frederick Bock, Oscar Blumenthal and Levinson. Often he conducts summer poetry workshops in Ireland, and is currently professor of English at Lehman College in New York.

Lee Cooper: *In 1950 my father convinced me to sit on the rail in front of the bear cage at the Detroit Zoo. A European brown bear paced behind me. Since 1974 I have lived and hiked in the mountains of Montana, Idaho and Washington, always aware of the bears who live and hike there too.*

Lisa A. Couturier, nature writer and poet, is grateful for the many glimpses of wild animals she's had on her travels through Indonesia and Latin American — as well as through her beloved urban lands of New York City. Her work appears in the anthologies *American Nature Writing 1998, The River Reader,* and numerous national magazines. She lives with her husband and daughter, along the Potomac River in Maryland.

Daphne Crocker-White: *I sleep with a three foot teddy bear every night (except when I travel he takes up too much room.) I then suffer a kind of withdrawal. I love to camp and am not afraid of the bears that wander through our stuff in the dead of night.* Crocker-White has been much published by *Encore Magazine, the Sarasota Review of Poetry, the Georgia State Poetry Society,* and many chapbooks. She has also won or placed in several small (or not so small) poetry contests. She lives in California.

Mary Crow is the Poet Laureate of Colorado. She is professor of English at Colorado State University and is widely published. Deeply engaged in the work of Latin and South American poets, she is translator of *Vertical Poetry: Recent Poems* by Roberto Juarroz; *From the Country of Nevermore*: poems by Jorge Teillier; and translator/editor of *Woman Who Has Sprouted Wings: Poems by Contemporary Latin American Women Poets* (which won a Translation Award from Columbia University's Translation Center.) She has received many writing awards including an NEA grant in poetry and a Fulbright Creative Writing Award. A book of her poetry, *I Have Tasted the Apple* was published by BOA Editions.

Ruth Daigon began her professional life as a singer, working with such luminaries as W. H. Auden to record Renaissance poetry and music, and as soloist with the New York Pro Musica. She sang at Dylan Thomas's funeral, then expanding to poetry, she founded, and was editor for twenty years of *Poets On:* She has been widely published in magazines, and on the Internet in over fifty *zines.* She has been Poet-Of-The-Month for the University of Chile's *Pares Cum Paribus.* Poetry awards include "The Eve of St. Agnes," 1993, (*Negative Capability*), The Ann Stanford Poetry Prize, 1997, and others. Her books include *Learning Not to Kill You, On My Side of the Bed, A Portable Past,* and most recently, *Between One Future and the Next.* Born and raised in Winnipeg, Canada, she now lives in California.

Dancing Bear is of Chippewa and Swedish ancestry. His poems, reviews and art have been published in many journal, including *New York Quarterly, Zuzu's Petals Quarterly, Slipstream, Pearl and Echoes*. He has been editor of a number of books and has two chapbooks: *From a Reconstructed Dream* and *Disjointed Constellations*. He lives in California.

Amy L. Dengler is a recipient of the Robert Penn Warren Award. Her work has appeared in *North Shore Magazine, Thema, Papyrus, Redrock Review, California Quarterly* and the *Anthology of New England Writers*. Her collection of poems, *Between Leap and Landing*, was recently published by Folly Cove. She lives in Massachusetts.

Jim DeWitt is editor of Eschew *Obfuscation Review, Free Fall Express, and Cephalic Thunder;* author of 14 books of stories and poems; managing editor of Pen-Dec Press, English Teacher emeritus and his writings have appeared in 1489 different literary publications. He has been nominated for a Pushcart Prize, won prizes and honors. He lives in Michigan.

Linda H. Elegant: *My grandparents owned a resort at Big Springs, Idaho, at the headwaters of the North Fork of the Snake River, very close to Yellowstone Park. When we stayed in the summers when I was a kid, bears were familiar and regular visitors. Later, I worked at Yellowstone and often saw a bear who lived nearby. I felt she was a real acquaintance, though not exactly a friend. I often saw her when I took a short cut. She napped in the same clearing every day.* Elegant teaches writing at Portland Community College, works on poems and stories and spends time outside as much as possible. She lives in Oregon where bears occasionally wander into the city from Forest Park, but not often.

S. C. Epstein: *When I think of bears, I think of the line by A. A. Milne, "A bear no matter how he tries, grows tubby without exercise." I am glad I have known bears that have come from happy homes. And thank all the wooden bears for their inspiration.* She lives in Connecticut.

Cathryn Essinger: *Although most of the bears in my life are invisible, they are nevertheless quite present. This has been a favorite poem of mine and , thematically, it is important in my collection, A Desk in the Elephant House, since it emphasizes how familiar things can become 'unfamiliar' in the right context.* Essinger teaches Creative Writing at Edison Community College. Her book won the Walt McDonald First Book Award in 1998, and her work has appeared in such journals as *Poetry, Poetry Northwest, Poetry Daily* and *Yankee*. She lives in Ohio.

David Allan Evans is Writer in Residence at South Dakota State University, currently on a second Fulbright Scholar grant teaching in Guangzhou, China. He has also won awards in creative writing from the NEA and the Bush Foundation of St. Paul. Of three poetry books, the latest is *Hanging Out with the Crows*, plus a nonfiction, *Remembering the Soos* about growing up in Iowa. *Although I have never encountered a real bear, I did learn when interviewing an Inuit, that polar bears are all left handed (pawed) and when stalking sometimes cover the black nose with a paw so nothing breaks the whiteness.*

Ella Eytan: *I grew up on a farm near Duluth, Minnesota where the bear was the black shoulder just slipping out of sight behind a thick fir, leaving a shoulder shaped emptiness. The bear was what you sang to, loud, so there would be no surprises, because you had to, simply had to wander those forests — cedar and pine, the peeling birches. The bear is more than itself. It is wound inextricably into our histories. Take it out and you are left with bear-shaped vacancies to stalk your nights.* Eytan is Co-Chair of the Marin Poetry Center and Editor of their Newsletter and anthologies. She has been widely published. She lives in California.

Sharon Fain: *I have been spending summer nights in bear country since the late forties, when my parents began a series of cross country trips in a station wagon filled with tents, cooking gear and four children. As a girl I felt happiest in the mountains — The Rockies, the Adirondacks, the Cascades.* Fain's work has appeared in *Poetry Northwest, Nimrod, the Literary Review, Southern Poetry Review, MidWest Quarterly* and in the book *Times Ten, An Anthology of Northern California Poets*. She lives in California.

Lyn E. Ferguson is the counselor at Triumph High School in Cheyenne, Wyoming, where she works with at-risk adolescents. She has observed and photographed wildlife in Africa, Costa Rica, Alaska, and throughout the rest of the United States. Her writing reflects respect for the gifts of nature and for diversity in the human condition. She often weaves the two themes together, sometimes accompanied by her photography. It is the intention of her work to create better understanding of universal human needs and the human spirit, and to inspire respect for the natural world.

David Smith-Ferri lives in California. His first book of poetry is *Into the Cauldron*, 1999. His poetry has most recently appeared in small press publications coming out of communities of faith and resistance, such as *Year One* and *Via Pacis*. He is a recent winner of the Soul-Making Literary Prize.

David Fisher: *"The Bear" is William Meredith's favorite poem of mine. He used always to read it at the Library of Congress.* Fisher won the first annual William Carlos Williams Award from the Poetry Society of America, and his *The Book of Madness* was nominated for a Pulitzer Prize. Fisher has 12 children and 5 grandchildren and having just remarried is in expectation of more. Fisher speaks and translates a number of languages, served in the Norwegian Merchant Marines, graduated *summa cum laude* from Duke University and now lives in California.

CB Follett is a Connecticut Yankee transplanted (successfully) in California. *Most of my bear experiences have been in Yosemite where with other families we made annual pilgrimages. I was majorly nervous when a mother bear somehow got between me and my three year old daughter. Neither of them were the least concerned, but I aged considerably.* Follett has been widely published, won some awards, some prizes and been nominated for five Pushcarts. She is the editor of Grrrrr and *Beside the Sleeping Maiden, Poets of Marin*. Her most recent poetry book, *Visible Bones*, was published in 1998.

Michael Foster *I collect (mostly) small, carved bears, particularly bear fetishes of the Native American tribes of the southwest. I think the impetus to collect bears and the impetus to write about them probably comes from the same place—but I don't know where that is.* Foster grew up in North Carolina. After two years in the Peace Corps in West Africa, he settled in the Atlanta area. His poems have appeared in a variety of publications including *International Poetry Review, Green Fuse, Rain Dog Review, Lynx Eye*, and *Slant*. He lives in Georgia.

Cynthia Gallaher: *The polar bear signifies how I feel about myself on good days; friendly, yet formidable.* Gallaher is a Green Team member for the Chicago Park District, educating the public about recycling and tree conservation. Her most recent book of poems is *Swimmer's Prayer*, 1999. "White on White" is part of an all-animal poetry manuscript entitled *Earth Elegance*.

Dana Garrett: *My camping friends often joke: "If you want to see a bear, go backpacking with Dana." Many bears have encountered me along the Appalachian Trail, particularly near the Delaware Water Gap area. I reside in the southern area of Lenapehocking: the original bioregion of the Lenape people to whom Bear is an important character. Through the study of Lenape lore and the close observation of bears, I have learned much about Bear and myself.* Garrett teaches philosophy and literature at Wilmington College. He also helps to coordinate a program that advocates for children in Delaware's foster-care system. He was the 1997 recipient of the Delaware Fellowship Grant in Poetry and his poetry has appeared in many journals.

J. Ruth Gendler is interested in living in a world where people are more creative, compassionate, and lively. This desire informs her creative work, including her art work, her teaching, and her books, *The Book of Qualities*, and *Changing Light*. She lives in California.

Dan Gerber: *From June to January I live on the Idaho/Wyoming border west of The Tetons where bears are a daily presence. I encounter their scat and tracks almost every day when I hike the nearby canyon to go fishing. Their* *proximity adds a rich and spooky dimension to our life. Occasionally, in late summer when Basque herders bring their flocks down from high pasture, I will see the ripped open body of a sheep and it makes me feel vulnerable and insignificant.* Gerber has published three novels and a book of short stories. His recent poetry collections are *A Last Bridge Home: New & Selected Poems* and the upcoming *Trying to Catch the Horses.*

Maria Mazziotti Gillan: *I am concerned by the destruction of the wilderness represented by the plastic bear in my poem. Bears, for me, are symbolic of the creatures who are lost and destroyed when every square inch of land is cemented over!* Gillan is the author of seven books of poetry, including *The Weather of Old Seasons* and *Things My Mother Told Me.* She is Founder and Director of the Poetry Center at Passaic County Community College and editor of the *Paterson Literary Review.* She has won numerous awards, including the May Sarton Award, two New Jersey State Council on the Arts fellowships, and a Chester H. Jones Foundation Award.

Rafael Jesús González is Professor Emeritus of Creative Writing & Literature at Laney College in Oakland, California. He is widely published in reviews & anthologies in the U.S., Mexico & abroad. His collection of verse is *El Hacedor De Juegos/The Maker of Games.* Also a painter, sculptor and installation artist, his work has been exhibited at the Oakland Museum, The Mexican Museum of San Francisco, the Charles Allis Art Museum, Milwaukee, and internationally. He was a Poet in Residence at the Oakland Museum & the Oakland Public Library in 1996.

Tzivia Gover works as a journalist and editor. Her articles have appeared in *The Boston Globe, The Advocate* magazine, *The Christian Science Monitor* and *Poets & Writers,* among others. Essays, stories and poetry have been in numerous anthologies and journals including *Love Shook My Heart, My Lover is a Woman, Malachite* and *Agate, Sinister Wisdom,* and *The Evergreen Chronicles.* She received her Master's of Fine Arts in writing from Columbia University. She lives in a corner of western Massachusetts known (for good reason) as Bear Mountain.

Taylor Graham: *We've never actually seen bear around here, but find their sign on our hikes and training. Recently, two of our handlers laid a trail and we ran the dogs on it half an hour later. There was a big pile of very fresh bear scat right in the middle of the path—our trail-layers swear it wasn't there when they passed through.* Graham trains and uses her dogs for Search and Rescue all over the country and her poetry has been widely published and awarded. She lives in the Sierra foothills of California.

Pamela Gray is a poet, screenwriter and playwright living in L.A., and a passionate lover of animals. *"the montana grizzlies" was based on a newspaper article that touched me deeply. In addition to a stressful screenwriting career, I am also a volunteer zookeeper at the Exotic Feline Breeding Compound in Rosemond, California, working towards the conservation of endangered big cats.*

Rasma Haidri: *Everything I know about bears came from my three year old daughter, creator of this poem, whose simple and clear wisdom taught me life's basic choice: you can fear the bear, or be the bear.* Haidri grew up in Tennessee, daughter of a Pakistani father and Norwegian-American mother. She spent most of her early adulthood in France and Norway. She has taught English and French, and is currently working as a Reading Specialist in Middleton, Wisconsin, where she is also a host for Radio Literature on public radio. She has won several prizes and been widely published.

Jim Hanlen: *Regarding my poem, when I went to the Portland, Oregon zoo, I was hoping some extraordinary, miraculous event would open up for me as it did for my wife.* Hanlen lives in Anchorage, Alaska.

Paul A. Hanson: *I bought a bear fetish from a catalog that described the bear fetish as protecting the wearer in travel, but I interpreted the description as protecting one from evil. I have worn it ever since and the bear, and the bear fetish have protected me from evils present, and travels taken. Entering the cave where the bear resides has led to a union: the drum beat, the heart beat, the bear and I have become one.* Hanson's poems have appeared in such publications as *Heeltap, Odyssey Orbital News, Muse of Fire,* and *Affair of the Mind, A Literary Quarterly.*

Jim Harrison: A reviewer for the *London Sunday Times* wrote, *Harrison is a writer with immortality in him*. He has written seven novels, the latest book being *The Road Home*, three novellas, eleven collections of poetry, innumerable essays, and screenplays. His books have been translated into 23 languages. He is a man of the outdoors and lives in a remote corner of Michigan.

Penny Harter: *I felt the power of bear on a camping trip in the Blue Ridge Mountains when one passed so near my camper window I heard its heavy breath and watched it lumber across the campsite clearing.* Harter has published fifteen books of poems, most recently *Turtle Blessing* and *Lizard Light: Poems From the Earth*, which celebrate the planet and the creatures who share it with us. Her work appears in numerous anthologies and magazines worldwide. She has won awards from the New Jersey State Council on the Arts, the Geraldine R. Dodge Foundation, and the Poetry Society of America. She lives and teaches in Santa Fe, New Mexico.

Juley Harvey: *Almost all of my favorite people are bears.* Harvey works at the Malibu Nite 'N' Day answering service to feed her poetry habit. She has been published in many magazines, interviewed on "Poetry Today" in New York City, and awarded prizes. She lives in California.

Marie Henry makes her lair in San Rafael, California. She is widely published including *Yellow Silk, Exquisite Corpse, Bite to Eat Place, Beside the Sleeping Maiden* and *Full Court: A Literary Anthology of Basketball*. She has fond memories of keeping her fifth-grade pens and pencils in a bear-shaped leather pouch.

Mary Kennan Herbert: *Last year in Hawley, Massachusetts, a bear showed up following a Fourth of July picnic in the woods, but to my great relief kept going, with a neighbor's dog in hot pursuit. Footprints and crushed ferns provided ample evidence that the ursine visitor was not imaginary. The bear population in western Massachusetts has increased in recent years.* Originally from Missouri, Herbert had a career as a senior editor in book publishing and now teaches writing courses at the Borough of Manhattan Community College. Within the last five years, over 100 of her poems have been accepted both nationally and internationally. She has two collections of poetry.

Jane Hilberry: *In the fall, before the bears went into hibernation, they had been very present around town. There were many signs warning about bears. I had a great desire and fear of seeing one. (None appeared) When I got home, I read a book about techniques for tracking bears, and then Crazy Jane stepped in and wrote the poem.* Hilberry was published in the *Denver Quarterly, Michigan Quarterly Review, Virginia Quarterly Review, The Journal*, and other magazines. Pearl Press published her chapbook, *Bad Girls*. She teaches at Colorado College.

Will Hochman is Director of Writing at the University of Southern Colorado, Poetry Editor of *War, Literature & the Arts*, and his poems have appeared in many small magazines and zines, and are collected in his two books, *Just Around the Corner and Stranger Within*. http://english/ttu.edu/kairos/2.2/toc.html# was named Webtext of the Year by Kairos. Hochman lives on Cheyenne Creek with his wife and a dog named "Holden Caulfield."

Jnana Hodson: *Each summer, bears sit on blueberry bushes as they pluck meals beside Contention Pond. Days later, the flattened shrubs tell me who's been visiting with the Quakers.* Jnana Hodson lives in New Hampshire.

Ted Hughes: Until his recent death, Mr. Hughes was the long-time Poet Laureate to Queen Elizabeth II. He is the author of more than forty books of poetry, prose, and translations, from *The Hawk in the Rain* to *Birthday Letters*. He recently won the Whitbread Prize for Poetry for his translation of *Tales from Ovid*. He lived in Devon, England.

Ingrid Jeffries finds much of her poetry inspired by the years she spent homesteading in Washington State and exploring what remains of America's "Wild West." She is a former firefighter for the U.S. Forest Service, and founded of Alaska's Kenai Trail. She is one of the founding editors of the Evergreen Women's Press and active in a performance troupe, which celebrates life's journeys through poetry. She is a member of the oral tradition in Jefferson County Public Schools and she lives in Colorado.

Paul Jenkins teaches poetry and poetry writing at Hampshire College and is editor of *The Massachusetts Review*. His first book, *Forget the Sky*, appeared in 1980; *Radio Tooth* in 1997. Father of two daughters, he lives with his wife in Massachusetts.

George Keithley admits to a long-time fascination with bears of many sorts. His most recent book of poems, *Living Again,* is published by Bear Star Press. His two pieces in this anthology are from a book of love poems, *The Burning Bear.* He is now at work on a book of essays about nature, which is titled *Black Bear Eating Salmon.* Poems have appeared in *Harper's, Agni, New Letters, Yale Review,* and *TriQuarterly.* He lives in California.

Diane Kendig: *I had a bear-shaped father who taught me to sing "The Teddy Bears Picnic." I saw my first bear in the Smoky Mountains. More recently, on a trip to Massachusetts, "The Fitchburg Bear" lumbered into town and inspired her poem published here.* Kendig is poet and translator, with two chapbooks, as well as grants and awards from the Ohio Arts Council, Yaddo, the NEH, and the Fulbright Association. She teaches at The University of Findlay in Ohio.

Kit Kennedy: *On my 45th birthday—ten years after my mother's death—I unexpectedly bought a silver bear pendant. Or, perhaps , this talisman "bought me."* Kennedy's work appears in the *Haight Ashbury Literary Journal, 33 Review* and the *Harvard Gay and Lesbian Review.* She has worked collaboratively (supplying the poem) with artist and print maker Donna Fenstermaker on the print, *Roses are Simple.* She lives in San Francisco.

Galway Kinnell has been highly honored and awarded. A former MacArthur Fellow, he has been State Poet of Vermont; Samuel F. B. Morse Professor of Arts and Science, and Erich Maria Remarque Professor of Creative Writing, both at NYU; director of an adult education program in Chicago; a journalist in Iran; and a field worker for the Congress of Racial Equality in Louisiana. Over many years, he has taught poetry at colleges and universities here and in France and Australia. His *Selected Poems* won both the National Book Award and the Pulitzer Prize. Kinnell has been called *the Walt Whitman of his generation.* His twelfth book of poetry, *Imperfect Thirst,* appeared in 1994.

Lynne Knight lives in Berkeley, California and works with a group of poets who published together in *Times Ten: An Anthology of Northern California Poets.* Her first collection is *Dissolving Borders* (QRL 1996.)

David Kubach says that *'Fellow Travelers" touches both the high points of his first 20 years of life: a bear out in the backyard one childhood summer in the Wisconsin woods, trail crew work among Montana grizzlies as a young man; it's been downhill ever since.* For the past 20 years, he has worked as a poet-in-residence for the Artist-in-Education programs of Wisconsin, Kentucky, Oklahoma, and both Dakotas. His poems have appeared in many journals. *First Things,* a collection, was published by Holmgangers Press. In the late seventies he helped found and edit a poetry magazine called *The Great Circumpolar Bear Cult.* He lives in Wisconsin.

Maxine Kumin has published eleven books of poetry, four novels, short stories, more than twenty children's books and three books of essays. She has received the Aiken Taylor Award for Modern Poetry, an American Academy of Arts and Letters award, the Sarah Joseph Hale Award, the Levinson Prize, a fellowship from the NEA, the Eunice Tietjens Memorial Prize and fellowships from the Academy of American Poets and the National Council on the Arts. She has served as Consultant in Poetry to the Library of Congress and as Poet Laureate of New Hampshire where she lives. Her latest poetry collection is *Connecting the Dots, 1996.*

Charlene Langfur is a writer of poetry and fiction, a college teacher and an organic gardener. She won a Womanspace award for her prose fantasy *Margaret's Song*, and was a finalist for the SUNY Paumanok Visiting Writers Awards. Her work has appeared in *Looking for Home*, *Literal Latté*, *Nebo* and others. She lives in the high mountain desert of Arizona.

Ralph La Rosa: *In Yosemite, while camping along the river beneath Half Dome, I felt hot breath and a rough tongue on my bare feet, which triggered an erotic dream, but awoke to find my dream lover, a large black bear, backing away from the tent flap and ambling to the river. Otherwise it has been the Bruins for ten years teaching at UCLA, and the Russian Bear as a Fulbright Scholar in the former Soviet Union.* La Rosa writes optioned feature and documentary film scripts, as well as literary essays and poetry. Recently he's *bearing* down on students at Los Angeles Mission College.

Gary Lawless is a practicing Caribouddhist from black bear country. He co-owns the Gulf of Maine Bookstore and publishes Blackberry Books. He has been widely published in places like *Green Fuse*, *Wild Earth*, and *Raise the Stakes*. He has written *Earth Prayers*, 1991, and *First Sight of Land*, 1990.

Ursula K. LeGuin: *My first name means Little Bear Woman, and I take it pretty seriously. My Kesh name is also Little Bear Woman — Intrumo — as I am a character in my own novel.* Born in California, now living in Oregon, she has received many awards for her more than forty books of fiction, poetry, criticism and children's stories. Her poem "The Bear's Gift" comes from the Kesh people of the Valley of the Na (where the poem was written.) The Kesh say that bears live in the Sixth House of the world, which is the house of rain and death. Her book *Always Coming Home* was runner-up for the National Book Award of 1984. She has recently published a translation of Lao Tzu's *Tao Te Ching* and a volume of new poems, *Sixty Odd*, will be published in 1999.

Joan Logghe has received many awards, among them the NEA, A Barbara Derning Grant and she was a finalist in the Western States Book Award. She has three books in print and three forthcoming. She lives in New Mexico.

Jeanne Lohmann: *I keep two carved soapstone bears on a kitchen ledge, reminders of legends, totems, fairytales — connections to mystery and power in BEAR!* Lohmann's most recent of five collections of poetry is *Granite Under Water* 1996, companion to her prose journal, *Gathering a Life*. *Between Silence and Answer, New and Selected Poems* was published in 1994. Her work, appearing in journals and anthologies is currently in *Wild Song*. She lives in Washington.

Denise Low: *I live with a bear. My husband, an enrolled member of the Menominee Nation of Wisconsin, is bear clan.* Low teaches creative writing and literature classes at Haskell Indian Nations University in Lawrence. She has published or edited a dozen books and chapbooks of poetry and personal essays. Forthcoming is *Selected Poems* from Penthe Press, and a book of prose poems, *A Daybook of Interiors*, from Haskell Foundation Press. She lives in Kansas.

Leza Lowitz: *In Native American medicine, Bear symbolizes the power of introspection. You can kill the bear, but the power used by shamans and mystics for centuries can never be tamed. I'm always looking in, so reaching out is the hardest thing to do. That's what saved me on the hunting trail of the Japanese mountain. We didn't trap any bears.* Lowitz is a poet, fiction writer and translator of Japanese poetry. A recipient of the PEN Syndicated Fiction Award and the Benjamin Franklin Award for Editorial Excellence, she has also received grants in translation from the NEA, the NEH, and, in poetry, from the California Arts Council. Her work has appeared in *Harper's*, *Ms.*, *Prairie Schooner*, *ZYZZYVA* and others. She is contributing editor to *Mānoa* and the *Japan Times*. She lives in California.

Seán Mac Falls was born in Boston and raised in Norfolk County, Massachusetts. He has since divided his time between America and Ireland, where he studied Celtic-literature and folklore, including some time spent at Trinity College, Dublin. His poetry has appeared in *Poetry Ireland*

Review, The Dominican College Review, Coracle, and *The Santa Barbara Review* among others. His most recent book is *Between the Leaves.* He is also a playwright and composer and has performed as a folk singer for over twenty years. He now lives in Port Angeles, Washington.

Elaine Magarrell lives in Washington DC and has published two volumes of poetry, *On Hogback Mountain* and *Blameless Lives.* Her poems have been widely published in anthologies, journals and text books. *I have experienced several sightings of bears in the wild. Last summer I saw a grizzly in Glacier National Park digging for something. What? A poem?*

Paul Mangan holds Master's degrees in English and Classics from the University of Iowa. He is a recipient of a New York Foundation for the Arts Poetry Fellowship and is director of The CCS Reading Series. His poems have appeared in such journals as *The Iowa Review, TriQuarterly, and The Virginia Quarterly.* Mangan works in an antiques store and teaches at Marymount Manhattan College. He lives in the West Village of New York City.

Peter Markus: *I briefly attended the University of Montana, home of the Grizzlies, though I never once encountered a real bear during my stay there.* Markus now lives in Michigan with his wife and two children, where the only bears he sees are those in the zoo.

Judith McCombs: *"The Man" came from an account of a Michigan auto worker whose life was scraping gravel all the way, who found the thrill of his lifetime in shooting a bear: his story changed, my mother and grandmother and Mother Nature came into it, and it became a poem of clashing archetypes, of woman allied with nature versus man against nature.* McCombs, born into a geodetic surveyor's family, grew up in almost all the continental United States. She is a teacher, has received several awards including a Neruda Award in *Nimrod,* a Maryland State Arts Council Award, Canadian Senior Fellowship, and an NEH. Her poems have been widely published. Among her books are three poetry books: *Against Nature: Wilderness Poems, Sisters & Other Selves,* and *Territories, Here & Elsewhere.* She lives in Maryland on the edge of wetlands and woods.

Ken McCullough is widely published and has received numerous grants and awards, among them the Academy of American Poets Award, an NEA Fellowship, a Pablo Neruda Award, a Galway Kinnell Poetry Prize, the Capricorn Book Award, a Witter Bynner Foundation grant and one from the Iowa Arts Council to continue translating the work of Cambodian poet U Sam Oeur. He and U are also translating Whitman's *Song of Myself* into the Khmer language, and he collaborated with Mark Bruckner on a chamber opera based on U's poems. McCullough's poetry books include *Travelling Light, Sycamore, Oriole,* and out this year, *Walking Backwards.* He teaches at Winona State University in Minnesota, and hikes and camps every year in the Beartooth Mountains of Montana and Wyoming, where he has had numerous bear affirmations.

Sally McNall: *In Yellowstone Park my four-year-old son and I watched a momma bear play with and teach her triplets for two hours from inside the VW minibus. No other encounter with a bear has matched that one, but it was formative.* McNall's concern for such beings is reflected in the title of her award winning chapbook *How to Behave at the Zoo and Other Lessons,* State Street Press, 1997. She has lived, taught and written in seven states, is a Pacific Northwesterner by birth and nature now living in California.

Robert Aquinas McNally: *An avid backpacker who is in the process of building a home in the mountains of far northern California. I chose the parcel in part because of the abundant bear signs.* He recently indulged his interest in bears by migrating to Churchill, Manitoba, at the same time that upwards of a hundred polar bears do the same thing. McNally is the author or co-author of six books of nonfiction, and his poetry has appears in a number of journals and anthologies. Currently he's writing a proposal for a book on polar bears.

Rich Mertes: *I first became enamored with bears after being chased by a merciful momma sow in Montana. For years thereafter, I was gifted with weekly bear dreams and occasional waking visions. Three years ago, after a prayer-*

filled request, I nervously enjoyed an actual bear hug from a wild bear in New Mexico. After dismissing his fifth graders at 3:30, he can usually be found on the first 'free Wednesday' of every month visiting his favorite prisoner in the San Francisco Zoo.

David Meuel's poetry collection, *Islands in the Sky,* received first prize for poetry in the *Writer's Digest* 1997 National Self-Published Book Awards. An avid backpacker, he has watched bears sniff inside his tent, eat his dinner, and do battle with food storage boxes. He lives in California.

A. A. Milne: At one time he was England's most successful, prolific, and best-known playwright. His *Toad of Toad Hall,* based on *The Wind in the Willows,* became a Christmas tradition and is still regularly produced. He also wrote two novels, one, well regarded *The House Mystery,* and he was an editor at *Punch,* but he is best known for his four books beloved by children of all ages. When Christopher Robin Milne was a year old, he was given a stuffed bear from Harrods, and later a tiger, a pig, and a donkey. The rest is history: *When We Were Very Young,* 1924, *Winnie-the-Pooh,* 1926, *Now We Are Six,* 1927 and *The House at Pooh Corner,* 1928.

Judith Minty: *I consider the bear my spirit guide and have had many encounters with him, both in dreams and in the waking world.* Author of nine books of poetry including *In the Presence of Mothers, Yellow Dog Journal,* and *Mad Painter Poems,* she lives in the North Woods of Michigan with her husband and her yellow dog. Her first book, *Lake Songs and Other Fears,* was recipient of the United States Award of the International Poetry Forum. *Walking With the Bear: Selected and New Poems* is her latest book.

N. Scott Momaday is a novelist, poet and painter. His books include: *The Way to Rainy Mountain, The Gourd Dancer* and *The Names.* He has received the Pulitzer Prize (*House Made of Dawn*) and the Permio Letterario Internazionale "Mondello," as well as the "Outstanding Indian of the Year Award," the Western Heritage "Wrangler" Award, the Distinguished Service Award by the Association of Western Literature and been named to the Oklahoma Hall of Fame. He is a Regents Professor of English at the University of Arizona and Visiting Professor of American Studies at the University of Regensburg, Germany. He lives in Arizona, is a member of the Kiowa Gourd Dance Society, and he is a bear.

Janell Moon is widely published and awarded. Her recent book of poems, *The Mouth of Home,* came out in 1999 from Arctos Press and her forthcoming book, *Wise Speaking: Writing as Spiritual Practice* is due in 2000. She writes, *I have sighted bears on many Hallowe'ens and in the Smoky Mountains.* She is a hypnotherapist and instructor, hails from Ohio and lives in California.

Miles David Moore: *I was a big fan of Yogi Bear as a child. I am also prone to growl at petty annoyances and have been known to destroy houses and cars in search of food.* He is a Washington correspondent for Crain Communications Inc. He performed at the 1993 National Poetry Slam in San Francisco and is founder and host of the Iota poetry reading series in Arlington, VA. He has won awards from *Poet Lore* and *Potomac Review* and has appeared in many other magazines.

Navajo People: (the Dine') The Navajo are the largest Indian tribe in the United States. Originally nomadic, they traveled from the Canadian North to the American Southwest more than 500 years ago, where they settled as farmers and herders of sheep, cattle and horses. They also trade in wool and hides and are known for their rugs and silver jewelry. The word Navajo comes from the Tewa, *navahu,* meaning "Cultivated Fields."

Duane Niatum was born and still lives in Seattle. His writings include essays on contemporary American Indian art and literature, two anthologies, *Carriers of the Dream Wheel* and *Harper's Anthology of Twentieth Century Native American Poetry,* five books of poetry with a new book, *The Crooked Beak of Love,* due out in 1999, plus two books making the rounds of publishers. He is an enrolled member of the Klallam tribe (Jamestown band).

Sheila Nickerson lived in Juneau, Alaska, for 27 years before leaving bear territory for the less wild coast of Washington. She had black bears visit her downtown property on a number of occasions but strove successfully to avoid bears on the trails and while picking berries; she owes this success to very loud and sometimes nonsensical conversations with family, friends and dogs. Her publications include *In the Compass of Unrest*, and *Feast of the Animals*.

Bill Noble once spent a memorable half hour in the Canadian Rockies in intimate face-to-face negotiations with a male grizzly about whether or not he might be food. "Sleep Warm" undoubtedly began to grow in his subconscious. His work has appeared in venues as varied as *convolvulus*, *Barnabe Mountain Review*, *Libido*, and *Paramour*. Noble is a naturalist and environmentalist in Marin County, California who has both communed and respectfully disagreed with bears from Nova Scotia to Alaska and the Sierra Nevada.

Doreen O'Brien: *The bear is my power animal, to which I've always felt deeply connected. I've seen black bears in Canada and in Michigan's Upper Peninsula but it was in a remote region of Alaska's Brooks Range that I was humbled first by a hole torn into the side of a hill where an Arctic squirrel had burrowed—and then the appearance of three grizzlies. I wrote "Mythos" with a sense of urgency the day hunting season opened.* O'Brien's work has appeared in *Peregrine*, the *New Press Literary Quarterly*, *The Silver Quill*, *Huckleberry Press* and the *Metro Times*. She lives in Michigan.

Celeste O'Dell: *My father and I were preparing to hunt mushrooms on his parents' homestead in the Elkhorn Mountains. We stopped to visit Mr. Sprague, who had lived for 40 years on the mountain. He said, "Well, the avalanche lilies are beginning to bloom and that means the bears are waking up. Be kind of careful. Bears wake up hungry."* O'Dell is primarily a fiction writer and recently won the Balch fiction prize from the *Virginia Quarterly Review*. Her play was produced this October by the Boulder, Colorado Museum of Contemporary Art. She lives in Oregon.

Mary Oliver's many awards include the Pulitzer Prize, the National Book Award, the Shelley Memorial Award, an Achievement Award from the American Academy and Institute of Arts and Letters, the Christopher Award and the *Boston Globe* Lawrence L. Winship Book Award, plus Guggenheim and NEA grants. She has eight books of poetry, including *House of Light*, *White Pine*, and most recently, *West Wind*, and three prose books, including *Blue Pastures*. Currently teaching at Bennington College, she lives in Massachusetts.

June Owens: *At age 8 I met my first bear while walking in Allegheny National Forest. An almost mystical mutual acceptance seemed to take place between that big, black bear and me. For a good distance we padded along in parallel about forty feet apart, now and then exchanging glances. Each time I paused to get a better look, the bear did the same. When I turned to go back, the bear continued on his way without so much as a backward Grrrr. I told my family; they didn't believe me.* Her latest poetry book is *treeline*, 1999. Owens now lives in Florida.

Nils Peterson has taught at San Jose State University since 1963 and coordinated the creative writing program for more than 20 of those years. He has published stories and articles on subjects from Shakespeare to golf. Publications include *Here Is No Ordinary Rejoicing* and *The Comedy of Desire*. He lives in California.

Robert Peterson is widely published. His latest book is *All the Time in the World*. Before that was *The Only Piano Player in La Paz*, and waiting in the wings is *Party of One: New, Found, and Selected Poems*. He lives in California.

Roger Pfingston is recently retired from teaching thirty-one years of English and photography at the secondary level. Some of his work has appeared in *New Letters*, *The Laurel Review*, *The Ledge* and *Barnabe Mountain Review*. No close encounters with bears except behind the lens of his camera. He lives in Indiana.

Naomi Rachel teaches Creative Writing at the University of Colorado. Recent publications include *Ribet! Frog Poems* and *The Muse Strikes Back*. She is Director of Residents Against Inappropriate Development (RAID) an activist group working to protect the ecological values of the Rocky Mt. Region. *I live up at 7,000 feet and commonly encounter bears. I've erected a 15' high steel bird feeding station operated with a boat winch so I can feed the birds without also feeding the bears.*

Bernice Rendrick was born in Kansas but has lived in Northern California for many years. As a senior she considers writing a luxury she can afford and indulges in it every day. She works with the Santa Cruz Writers Union poetry group on projects and has published recently in *The Rockford Review, Quarry West, Santa Barbara Review* as well as several anthologies.

Carlos Reyes: *The first bear I saw was a very large and black creature standing on his hind legs casually having a lunch of rose hips on the Colville Reservation in Washington. He is not the bear in the poem.* Reyes has also worked in native communities in Nevada, Arizona and Alaska such as Inchelium and Nespelem. He frequently travels to Ireland where he maintains a 19th century cottage. He is widely traveled, widely published, has received awards, residencies, edited literary reviews and was the editor and publisher of Trask House Books, Inc. Recent books of poetry: *A Suitcase Full of Crows*, 1995, and *Oilean Agus Oilean Eile* ("Two Islands") forthcoming. He lives in Oregon.

Martha Rhodes is a founding editor of Four Way Books and director of the CCS Reading Series at Civic Center Synagogue in New York City where she lives. She holds an MFA from Warren Wilson College and her poems have appeared in *Agni, Bomb, Harvard Review, Ploughshares, Quarterly West, The Virginia Quarterly Review* and others.

Adrienne Rich has taught at many of our finest universities and currently at UC Santa Cruz in California. She has gathered a rich collection of laurels: the Yale Younger Poets Series, two Guggenheim Fellowships, Amy Lowell Traveling Fellowship, Ruth Lilly Poetry Prize, LA Times Book Prize, Lenore Marshall/Nation Prize, the Frost Silver Medal for distinguished lifetime achievement, the National Poetry Association Award for Distinguished Service to the Art of Poetry and the Tanning Award for Mastery in the Art of Poetry. She has published over fifteen books, among them *Diving into the Wreck*, co-winner of the National Book Award for Poetry, *An Atlas of the Difficult World*, finalist for the National Book Award and Nation Book Critics Circle Award. In 1994 she was named a MacArthur Fellow. Her latest poetry book is *Midnight Salvage*, 1999.

Melanie Richards is a poet and prose writer with recent work in *Yankee, The Harvard Review, Shenandoah, Negative Capability* and elsewhere. She won the 1995 Sue Saniel Elkind National Poetry Prize from Kalliope judged by Joy Harjo. She lives in Minnesota.

Elliot Richman: *What happens in my poem "A Black Bear" is what I saw.* Richman's publications include: *Honorable Manhood, Poems of Eros & Dust, Walk On Trooper,* and *The World Dancer.* He has won an NEA and a NYFA. He lives in New York.

John Rowe grew up in the neighboring cities of Albany (where he now lives) and Berkeley, California. He has worked in a family retail business, been a teacher and is currently employed with a licensed sound contractor in Oakland. He is president of the Bay Area Poets Coalition and co-editor of *Poetalk* magazine.

Mary Rudge went to school with and was influenced by friends of the Indian Nation in Oklahoma, western artists and writers in Texas and California, studied in Mexico, won grants and awards. She writes and speaks for global peace education, environmental concerns, intercultural understanding and the impact of poetry and creativity on social change. She lives in California.

Kay Ryan lives in California and teaches writing at the College of Marin. Her poems have appeared in *The New Yorker, Atlantic, New Republic, Paris Review, Georgia Review, Yale Review* and others.

Publications include *Strangely Marked Metal* and *Flamingo Watching* from Copper Beech Press and her most recent, *Elephant Rocks,* Grove 1996.

Leonard Sanazaro teaches English, Classics and Creative Writing at City College of San Francisco. He is literary executor for the Estate of William Dickey. Poems have appeared in *Tennessee Quarterly, The Centennial Review, Antioch Review* and *The Denver Quarterly.*

John Savant, recently retired as professor of English at Dominican College, has also taught literature at Carysfort College in Dublin, Ireland. In 1991, Savant was recipient of the Cate Award for Excellence in the Teaching of College English and was recently honored by Dominican with the first annual Sarlo Distinguished Professor of the Year Award. His poems have appeared in *The Southern Review, Sequoia, The Journal of Irish Literature, The Furrow* (Ireland) and elsewhere. His most recent book is *Brendan's Voyage & Other Poems.* He lives in the San Francisco Bay Area.

Dan Schneider lives in Minnesota.

Delmore Schwartz was a lifelong baseball enthusiast and a great fan of the New York/San Francisco Giants. He began his rise in the New York intellectual circle of poets with his book, *In Dreams Begin Responsibilities,* 1938. He won the Bollingen Prize in Poetry and the Poetry Society of America's Shelley Memorial Award. Other books include: *The Ego is Always at the Wheel, I Am Cherry Alive, Magic of Thinking Big* and *Last and Lost Poems of Delmore Schwartz.*

Gail Shafarman: *I wrote this piece after a trip to the Queen Charlotte Islands, and I hope it conveys some of the mystery (and sexy humor) of the those cultures (and ours).* Dr. Shafarman practices and lives in the San Francisco Bay Area.

William Sheldon: *As a child living in Montana, I grew up with contradictory images of bears. One from watching them eating marshmallows from the hands of tourists in Yellowstone. The other from stories like that of "Grizzly." Eventually, the latter image became more instructive, not for its "bogeyman" qualities, but because it is a reminder of our need for humility.* Sheldon now lives and teaches in Kansas. Poems have appeared in such magazines as *Angelflesh, Blue Mesa Review,* and *Organization and Environment.*

John E. Smelcer: *I was briefly mauled by a bear many years ago and still have the scars to prove it.* Poetry editor at *Rosebud* and at *Salmon Run Press,* Smelcer lives in Alaska. His poems have appeared in *The Atlantic Monthly, The Kenyon Review* and *Amicus.* His most recent book of poetry is *Changing Seasons.* He has written widely of Native American myths and literature including *The Raven and the Totem, A Cycle of Myths, In the Shadow of Mountains, Indian Stories,* and most recently editing the anthology, *Durable Breath: Contemporary Native American Poetry.* He is the last speaker/writer of two Native American languages and the author of one dictionary and another in progress.

Claude Clayton Smith: *I am Professor of English at Ohio Northern University and our mascot is the Polar Bear. I am currently editing and translating, with Alexander Vaschenko of Moscow State University, the first English language edition of Native Siberian Literature, many of which feature the bear, including an account of the Bear Feast, a sacred ritual in which the bear visits from the forest, is royally treated with myth-songs, then "danced" home.* Smith is the author of five books, editor of a sixth and his work has been translated into five languages, including Russian and Chinese.

Laurence Snydal: *I lived for many years on the Klamath River in northern California and there I met Bob and heard his story. Regularly, black bears used to raid our plum thicket on Indian Creek in the fall.* Snydal's poetry has appeared in such magazines as *Blue Unicorn, Caperock, Lyric* and *Gulf Stream.* Publications include *The New Fathers Survival Guide,* 1987. He lives in California and is poet, cook and musician.

Gary Snyder has worked on the docks, worked in the engine room of a tanker, and lived for many years in Japan, where he studied Buddhist philosophy and did research and translations of

Zen texts. During the 50s he was a part of the San Francisco Beat movement. After he and Kerouac climbed Matterhorn Peak in the Sierra, Kerouac used Snyder as the model for Japhy Ryder in *Dharma Bums*. He has published sixteen books of poetry and prose and *Turtle Island* received a Pulitzer Prize. Other poetry books include *Mountains and Rivers without End, Axe Handles*, and *Left Out in the Rain*. Snyder teaches literature and wilderness thought at the University of California–Davis, and lives in the Sierra foothills.

Laura Snyder lives in Seattle, but confesses her heart-home ("Bear Paw") is 80 acres in the wilds of British Columbia. She rambles the forests where she grew past her fear of the wild, but wears a bear-bell necklace and carries a stout walking stick. *I think of myself as a naturalist who writes.* Ten writing awards and many publication credits have mushroomed since she began writing midlife in 1992. She says that *"The Bear" by Galway Kinnell was one of the most influential poems which got her started writing.*

Soldier Blue: *Smoke + / shadows / buried in the / moonlight / my brother / calls / + I answer / the darkness / is our shelter / our rough paw prints / + claw-mark trees / are the landscape / scars / on this our heart land / The pulse of Earth Mother / is ours to hear / her heart beat / is our map / My Brother + I / bonded by blood / to the bear clan.* (drum song) Soldier Blue, of Grande Osage Nation and Eastern Cherokee descent on his father's side and German, Scot, and Welsh on his mother's side, lived for his first six years in Guatemala. He writes his poetry in both Spanish and English and performs with music and without. He works for Continental Airlines and lives in Houston. *I raise a toast to us all & give thanks to Grandfather Spirit & Wakan Tanka.*

Judith Sornberger: *My mother never recovered from bear fear after reading "Night of the Grizzlies" years ago, but I haven't inherited her fear and find that instead I am fascinated by bears and always hope to see them on my walks beside the Tioga River.* Poetry collections include *Open Heart, Calyx, Judith Beneading Holoferenes* and *Bifocals Barbie: A Midlife Pantheon*, both from Talent House. She lives in Pennsylvania.

t. kilgore splake lives on michigan's frozen upper peninsula "pictured rocks" area and fights 'alberta clippers' bare chested. his poetry titles include *last train out, jim-jack fevers, trout dancing sonata, the porcupine mountains papers*, and most recently, *opening day breakfast memories*.

Hannah Stein: *The first book read to me as a small child was a flowery poem called "Honey Bear," whose first few pages I could easily be persuaded to recite from memory.* She lives in Davis, California where she writes, teaches poetry workshops, and edits, along with a few others, *americas review*. Poems have appeared in *Poetry Northwest, Poetry Flash, Prairie Schooner*, and in a chapbook published by State Street Press, *Schools of Flying Fish*. Fish but no bears.

Robert Sward: Winner of a Guggenheim Fellowship, Sward is author of *A Much-Married Man, A Novel*, and *Four Incarnations, New & Selected Poems*. His *34 Poets Named Robert* won the 1990 Villa Montalvo Literary Arts Award. He has taught at Cornell, University of Victoria, B.C., at the Iowa Writers' Workshop, and currently treaches in Santa Cruz, California. Winner of the WebScout's Way Cool Site Award for editing eSCENE 1996, (www.cruzio.com/~scva/rsward.html). Sward has contributed to over 300 literary journals and e-zines.

Susan Terris: *Once at 2 am in the wilds of northern Minnesota, I chased a bear while brandishing a small Boy Scout hatchet. I have elected not to write a poem about this moment of madness.* Terris' book *Curved Space*, 1998 La Jolla Poets Press, is joined by two published even more recently: *Eye of the Holocaust*, Arctos Press and *Angels of Bataan*, Pudding House Publications. Her poems have appeared in many literary magazines and she is the recipient of many awards and prizes. She lives in San Francisco.

Madeline Tiger: *I have five grandsons. I sing them the old songs. We say poems. We give each other the ancient stories, all new. I have carried poems all my life. Now I go all over the country to visit my scattered family. At every* *intersection there is a brightness rising. Inside is the secret that no one will tell. I have used Momaday's folktale of the bear/boy and the 7 sisters many times in teaching Poetry in the Schools, but no student ever asked what happened to the bear, only my grandson, Victor.* Tiger's most recent books are *Water Has No Color, Mary of Migdal,* and *My Father's Harmonica.* She lives in New Jersey.

Yuri Vaella (Aivaseda) was born in the village of Veriegan in West Siberia. He is of the taiga Nenets people, who historically moved south from the tundra to the taiga forest and adopted the culture of the Khanty "reindeer people." Poet and reindeer owner, his poetry appears in leading Russian literary magazines. His collection of poems, *White Cries,* was published in Surgut in 1996.

Kay Van Natta: *I've always loved bears. Maybe it's the power and beauty. Maybe it's how funny they can be, or their casual certainty that the realms they walk are most surely theirs to rule. I've seen the occasional black bear strolling the woods of Michigan, brown bears in Alaska, and in Montana the territorial hash marks cut into the side of a ranger's cabin way over my head (and I was on a horse at the time!)* Van Natta is a teacher in Michigan. This will be her first published poem.

Donna J. Waidtlow: *As a child I was always awaiting the arrival of gypsies. They never came – so at eighteen I began a decade of roaming the arctic, living at Wild Lake, the Alatna River, the Kanuti Kilolitna River and summers in Fairbanks. Grizzly bears were part of the fabric of my life.* Her poetry has been published in *Alaska Quarterly Review, Anima, Avocet, Paper Boat, Potato Eyes* and others. Her book, *A Woman Named Wife,* won the Floating Bridge Press Chapbook Contest. She lives in Washington.

Sharon Rose Waller grew up in Denver where one of her first friends was a stuffed bear named "Bear." After living in various cities throughout the world she is now semi-settled in Albany, California and works with graduate students at UC Berkeley (Go Bears!) She has continued to have a deep connection with both real and imagined bears.

Daniel J. Webster published his book *Dreams and Responsibilities* in 1993, about $2/3$rd his own poetry and $1/3$rd translations from German and Russian. He also has a chapbook, *Fir and Birch* and has published several articles introducing Eastern European literature in editions of *Printed Matter.* Webster lives in Japan.

Anthony Russell White: *My teddy is named Running Bear, after the song I identified with so strongly in the 1960s. He travels everywhere with me, including camping and fishing trips. He carries a small yellow backpack with his pillow, some poems to read, and his sacred objects. Running Bear does not like to bath in the whirling machine, but submits to it with dignity.* White and Running Bear live in California.

J. D. Whitney: *"Grandmother (wakes)" is from a 57 poem sequence called What Grandmother Says, spoken in her voice (as creator, co-creator, shape-shifter, trickster), in which Bear is an important character.* Whitney lives in Wisconsin.

Daniel Williams: *I am one of the "Sons and Daughters of John," those of us who have followed in Muir's footsteps and have lived and written about the Sierra Nevada. The Southern Sierra Miwok (the Ahwahnichee) of Yosemite Valley consider the bear, especially the grizzly, to be right up there with Osiris, Dionysis, Christ and other "fisher king" or fertility deities. The first week in June is the great celebration of the "coming out of bear," in which the reappearance into the world of the bear after his winter torpor is celebrated. This is observed with feasting and dancing and especially the "bear dance," which is a magical commemoration of the cyclical renewal of strength and spirit in the world. This is a dance of great power for physical and spiritual renewal.* Williams lives near Yosemite in Wawona.

Paul Willis is Professor of English at Westmont College in Santa Barbara, California. His poems have appeared in *Poetry, Petroglyph, Wilderness* and *Best American Poetry 1996. Veteran of many heroic encounters, I once scared a bear so badly in Tuolumne Meadows that it peed all over the backseat of my friends' van.*

Christopher Woods: *I was very impressed to learn, in adolescence, while on vacation in Gatlinburg, Tennessee, that bears like "Smokey" were for real.* Woods is a native Texan who writes fiction, non-fiction, poetry and plays. His work has appeared in over 300 publications including *New England Review, Columbia, The Southern Review* and *Short Story International*. His plays have been produced, his novels published and he has taught writing at Rice University Continuing Studies and at The Women's Institute.

Bill Yake: *I encountered my first grizzlies (a sow and cub) at about 20 yards in 1965 while doing trail work in Glacier National Park.* More birds than bears now inhabit Yake's poems which have appeared in *Wilderness Magazine, Least Loved Beasts of the Really Wild West: A Tribute, Duckabush Journal,* and *convolvulus.* His latest chapbook, *The Faces of Birds,* recounts experiences in Papua, New Guinea where no bears observe amazing birds. He lives in Washington.

Kristin Camitta Zimet: *Known as CB (Cuddly Bear), I live with my husband John HMB (Hug-Me-Bear) in the Shenandoah Valley of Virginia. Hiking in fog on the first day of our honeymoon, we came face to face with a pair of bears atop Mt. Leconte. I work as a naturalist and have had the good fortune to observe bears in the wild more peacefully since.* CB's poems have appeared recently in *Primavera, Centennial Review, Appalachian Journal, Riverwind* and her first collection of poetry, *Take in My Arms the Dark* was published in 1998 by Sow's Ear Press.

The Artists

Cover Art from a photograph by **Alessandra De Clario**, Ph.D. Animal activist and environmentalist, and always an artist, her art has moved into filmmaking, video, and photography. Using a light box, she creates a back-lit effect, which provides additional drama to the finished work. She uses a universe sky background in most of her work because it's her way of expressing the connection with everything—the ultimate eco-system. She follows the Buddhist concept *Esho-Funi,* which basically means you and your environment are one. Her piece, *The Illuminating Reality Woman of the Universe,* was chosen for the main conference room of the Women's Clinic and Family Counseling Center in West Los Angeles. She lives on the coast in California.

Robyn Bergsma's art originally appeared with the poem "Out Picking Berries."

JoAnn Burchfiel: *One evening, camping in Yosemite we went to sleep under the stars. But we forgot to close a window in our car and a big bear slipped right in and ate every morsel of our food. We watched without moving and when finished, she slipped out again and wandered off, leaving not a crumb of granola, not a scratch, nothing out of place. Considerate and neat bear, eh?* Burchfiel is a calligrapher, photographer, teacher and volunteer. She has received awards and commissions and conducts her art under the title Letters & Images. She lives in California.

Laura Corsiglia was raised in northern British Columbia's Nass Valley surrounded by grizzly bears. Her first art experiences were the masks, dances, songs, and totem poles of the Nisga'a indigenous people for whom her parents worked. Extensive traveling and an education at Paris' École Nationale Superieure des Beaux-Arts added an international element to her respect for Bears in all forms. She has exhibited her paintings in Paris, Vancouver and Kyoto—spreading a profound appreciation for Bears both actual and spiritual.

CB Follett is a poet, editor and artist.

Phil Frank lives in California. His comic strip "Farley" appears six times a week in the *San Francisco Chronicle.* Among other scenarios, one of the most popular is that of the bears of Yosemite, who run a seasonal diner, the Fog City Dumpster, in San Francisco. One of those bears, Alphonse, is a devoted, and sometimes anguished, Giants fan. Among his published books, Mr. Frank has two about to appear from the Yosemite Association: *The Bear Facts,* illustrated, the story of the black and brown bears of the Lower 48, and *Fur and Loafing in Yosemite,* a book from his comic strip world, many of which feature the bears. Using his artwork, he works with the Bear Management Staff to show proper behavior around bears.

Joyce Livingston has been a professional fine artist most of her adult life. She studied art in Portland, OR, majored in art and architecture at the University of Oregon, attended the Pasadena School of Fine Arts and studied with many prominent artists. She has had many solo shows, taught and given workshops, is a painter, printmaker, and does mixed media works. She lives in California where she is both poet and painter.

N. Rudin did the frontispiece for David Fisher's book *Teachings.* Her work accompanies his poem in GRRRRR.

E. H. Shepard is the reknowned illustrator of many of the books of A. A. Milne. They met when both were working at *Punch,* where Ernest Shepard was a *Punch* illustrator. Always interested in art, Shepard attended the Royal Academy Schools as one of its youngest students. Besides the illustrations for Milne's books, Shepard is also know for his illustrations in Kenneth Grahame's *The Wind in the Willows,* among others. One of Graham Shepard's toys, a teddy bear named Growler, was the model for Winnie-the-Pooh, for Shepard felt that his sketches of Christopher Robin's bear weren't quite right.

David Graber graciously wrote one of the comments for the back cover. Dr. Graber spent more than a decade studying the ecology and behavior of black bears in the Sierra Nevada. He is a scientist with the National Park Service in Sequoia and Kings Canyon National Parks.

Bears walk with their entire sole on the ground (plantigrade), as do humans. This allows them to stand upright. They move both legs on one side, then both on the other, giving them a lumbering gait. They place the hind foot into the print left by the fore foot, and so will each following bear, thus creating trails that last for years. They are fast for short distances and most can easily climb trees. They have five toes with curved non-retractable claws, usually longer on the hind feet. They are capable swimmers. Most are largely vegetarian. They have excellent eyesight with good depth perception and some form of color vision, excellent hearing, and a sense of smell as keen as a bloodhound's. When on their hind legs it is often to facilitate their scent gathering. They are very curious and good learners. The lips of bears are not attached to their gums allowing great mobility and protrusion, and their teeth have growth rings like trees. Their skeletons are similar to ours. With hibernating bear species, delayed implantation allows the embryo to wait until hibernation to attach to the uterine wall, and cubs are born while the mother is still in hibernation. Newborn cubs are blind, toothless, hairless and about the size of chipmunks. During hibernation, bears will neither pass urea or solid fecal waste. The urea is recycled into usable proteins. Emerging from hibernation, bears are lethargic for several weeks while their metabolism rebuilds.

Family *Ursidae* ꙮ Bears

Ursinae ꙮ Old and New World, Pleistocene–Recent

Agriotheriinae ꙮ Eurasia, Miocene–Pliocene

Tremarctinae ꙮ North and South America, Pliocene–Recent

Ailuropodinae ꙮ western China, Pliocene–Recent

Old World Bears of Europe and Asia (extinct)

Amphicyon: Oldest ancestor of the bears, early Miocene (approximately 25 million years ago), shows characteristics of both bears and dogs, which confirms the evolutionary relationship between these two groups. (extinct)

Ursavus: Considered to be the first actual bear, middle Miocene (22-20 mya). (extinct)

Agriotherium: A more bear-looking fossil species, late Miocene (18-15 mya). (extinct)

Protursus: Considered the ancestral species to most of our living bear species. (extinct)

Ursus spelaeus: The Cave Bear. Gigantic bear probably closely related to, or an ancestor of, the brown bear. Northern Europe and Asia, early Glacial to late Pleistocene (500,000 to 10,000 years ago). (extinct)

Current European and Asian Species

Ursus arctos: The brown bear–most widespread distribution of the bear species, found throughout most of the northern hemisphere, limited in much of its original range by the reduction of mountain forests. The brown bear still exists in Eurasia, and a population of brown bears lives on the Japanese island of Hokkaido. Those left in Europe are mostly in remote mountain woodlands. There are many sub-species of *Ursus arctos*, but scientists are not yet in agreement on their classifications. (threatened)

Ailuropoda melanoleuca: The giant panda of Southwest China. Perhaps the most primitive of the bears. It is white with black eye patches, ears, legs, band across shoulders, lips and has an unusually large head. Lives mainly on the ground though can climb trees. Does not hibernate but goes to lower elevations for winter and spring. Has especially adapted molars and throat for crushing and withstanding the sharp splinters of bamboo, which it eats almost exclusively. Has an enlarged wrist bone that works as an opposable thumb. Quite vocal and mostly nocturnal. Reduction in range and periodic die-offs of bamboo threatens its existence. (endangered)

Helarctos malayanus: The sun bear (also Malay or honey bear) inhabits lowland tropical forests of southeast Asian from Malaysia and Indonesia almost to India. Smallest of the bears, with a U-shaped breast mark in whitish or orange and with grayish or orange muzzle, long strongly curved and pointed claws, bowed legs. Its hairless soles make a better grip for climbing, as they live mainly in trees. They do not hibernate. (endangered) (now extinct in India, Bangladesh; in dire straits in Burma, Thailand, Laos, Kampuchea and Vietnam)

Melursus ursinus: The sloth bear is covered with a long, shaggy black coat especially across the shoulders. It has a distinctive white or yellowish chevron on its chest. Lips are protrusible and mobile, naked snout is mobile, nostrils can be closed, inner pair of upper incisors missing; with these tools it can suck termites (its favorite food) like a vacuum. This noise can be heard up to 200 yards away. Also eats fruit, honey, and other plants and although not predatory by nature, sloth bears will eat carrion when found. (vulnerable)

Selenarctos thibetanus: The Asiatic black bear lives predominantly in deciduous forest and brushy areas in mountainous regions of southern Asia, as well as southeastern Russia, Taiwan, and the Japanese islands of Honshu and Shikoku. A medium-sized, black (sometimes brown) bear with lightish muzzle, oversized ears and a distinct white patch on the chest usually in the shape of a V, with white on the chin. Mainly nocturnal, it sleeps in trees or caves. Frequently makes crude leafy feeding platforms in nut-bearing trees, but has a wide range of foods, both plant and small animals. (endangered)

New World Bears

came to North American about 1.5 mya across the Bering land mass.

Arctodus: The short-faced bear. Late Pleistocene (500,000 to 10,000 years ago). Probably one of the largest bears with comparatively long legs and great speed. (extinct)

> *Arctodus pristinus*: Lesser Short-faced Bear (extinct)

> *Arctodus simus*: Giant Short-faced Bear (extinct)

Tremarctos floridanus: The Florida cave bear lived in Florida and along the Gulf Coast, New Mexico and northern Mexico. Associated with black bears. (10,000 to 8,000 years ago). (extinct)

Ursus abstrusus: Primitive black bear (early Pliocene 13,000 to 2,000 years ago). (extinct)

Ursus etruscus: Ancestral form of brown bear (extinct)

Current North American Species

Ursus arctos: The brown bear lives in meadows and open areas. May be dark brown, some red, cream or black. The long hairs on shoulders and back may be frosted white, hence grizzled. They have long fore claws not adapted for tree climbing. A large brown bear can outrun a horse.

> *Ursus arctos middendorffi*: The Alaskan brown (Kodiak) bear, coastal Alaska, British Columbia, and offshore islands. Broad skull. (Relatively common in Western Canada and Alaska) (threatened in continental USA)

> *Ursus arctos dalli*: The Alaskan brown bear, Alaskan peninsula into coastal British Columbia. Narrow skull.

> *Ursus arctos horribilis*: The Grizzly bear, usually inland areas of Alaska, and throughout the Rockies of North America. (threatened in lower 48 states)

>> *Ursus arctos californicus*: The California grizzly; coastal and interior areas of California, possibly into Oregon and Baja California (recently extinct)

Ursus arctos nelsoni: The Mexican grizzly, mountains and foothills of southern New Mexico, Arizona, northern and central Mexico. (recently extinct)

Ursus americanus: The black bear, restricted to North American forests, swims and climbs well. Black pelage, some cinnamon or chocolate brown, with brown muzzle, may have white chest patch, Western North America; pale blue (Glacier bear), South Alaska; white or yellowish white, Pacific coast of central British Columbia. (declining but still common in Alaska, Canada and much of the conterminous United States. Other populations are threatened or endangered.)

Ursus americanus floridanus: Mostly in Florida (extinction imminent)

Ursus americanus kermodei: (Ghost bear) nearly white with brownish muzzle. Lives on three small isolated islands off the coast of British Columbia.

South American Bear

Tremarctos ornatus: The spectacle bear lives in a wide range of habitats in northern South America, all of which contain bromeliads and fruits, their preferred food, though they will eat a variety of small animals, and other plants. Black, may be brown, with circular or semicircular creamy white "spectacles" around the eyes, and a variety of markings on the throat and chest. Constructs tree nests as feeding and sleeping platforms. (threatened)

Polar Region Bear

Thalarctos maritimus: The polar bear is found in all of the polar regions of the northern hemisphere, including Russia, Norway, Greenland, the United States and Canada. Preferring areas where the northern seas meet the shorelines, it follows the pack ice of the Arctic Circle. Crisscrossed with fingerlets of open water called leads, caused by constant freezing and thawing of ice, this is also the preferred habitat of the seal. Largest land carnivore, the polar bear's favorite food is the ringed seal, which it can smell from twenty miles away, and it will stand by a seal hole fifty hours at a stretch. When stalking it may cover its black nose. This long-necked bear has an undercoat of fine white hair covered by long guard hairs which are hollow, allowing for greater water buoyancy. Its skin is black to absorb as much heat as possible. Webbed fore paws allow it to swim about 6 mph, and it can swim 50 miles of open water. The hind paws act as rudders. When endangered, a polar bear cub may bite onto its mother's tail and be towed to safety. The polar bear can submerge up to two minutes, dive to 15 feet, closing its ears and nostrils, and leap 7 to 8 feet in the air to catch a resting seal. The bottoms of its feet are covered with dense hair and vacuoles that act as suction cups for ice traction. (vulnerable)

International Bear

"Ursus americanus roosevelti": American Teddy Bear, wide range of colors, found on all continents, mixes freely with humans. Not known to consume food. Fully domesticated. (common)

exit, pursued by a bear.

Naming the Bear

Spirit Names for the bear

Many native tribes consider the bear too sacred to call by name and instead give the bear synonymic titles, some of which follow:

Ainu	The Divine One Who Rules the Mountains
Blackfoot	Big Hairy One
Cree	Memekwesiw–spirit boss of all the bears (a bear is, therefore, Memekwesiw's Little Pup)
	Short Tail
	Black Food
	Big-Great-Food
	Angry One
	Sticky Mouth
	That Big Hairy One
Estonians	Broad-foot
Finns	Apple of the Forest (also Michikaman)
Blackfoot (and many tribes)	Bobtail
	Bog Feet
	Pride of the Woodlands
	Glory of the Wilderness
	Honey-eater
	Famous Lightfoot
	Blue-Tail
	Snub Nose
Koyukon	Black Place
	Dark Thing
	The Animal
Lapps	The Old Man with the Fur Garment
Northwest (and many tribes)	(ch tik tek) Those that go down to the sea (polar bear)
	The Old One
	Four Legged Human

Ostyak	Dweller in the Wilds
Yukaghir	Owner of the Earth Great Man
Zuni	Master of the West Coat the Color of the Land of Night Aincekoko–Zuni bear kachina
(Others)	Fine young chief
	The Dog of God
	Reared in the Mountains
	Food for the Fire
	The Blue Tooth
	The One Who Goes
	The One Who Owns the Chin
	Cousin
	Grandmother
	Big Great Food
	The One Who Goes Around in the Woods
	That Which Went Away
	Supernatural One
	The Great Lonely Roamer (polar bear)
	Coat the Color of Night
	Honey Paws
	Pride and Beauty of the Forest
	Grandfather

Some Earthmother-bear archetype names

Nez Perce	Bearwoman (Grizzly)
Yavopai and Navajo	Bearwoman with Toothed Vagina
Tlingit, Kaska, Tagish	Zuts Tla (Bear Mother)